IN APPRECIATION

A special THANK YOU to the members and friends of Shepherd's Fold Baptist Church of Hutchinson, Minnesota for their patience with me in the unfolding and development of the truths contained in this book. You have helped me to grow through these studies. God blessed in the many decisions that you made to the glory of God during the preaching of this series. It has also been a blessing to see the increase of spiritual fruit through your lives as you began to implement the doctrine of Grace into the practice of your everyday lives.

I also want to thank Mrs. Julie Rydberg for her careful and meticulous proofreading of the manuscript. I pray our Lord will bless you in a special way for your generosity in giving many hours to this work.

To my wife, Patty – thank you for your patience in allowing me almost every free moment of our lives together for the last two years to finish this work. You catered to my every need so as to allow me the time I needed. Your graciousness has exemplified all the truths defined by the doctrine of Grace. Your self-sacrificing love reveals the selflessness that manifests the Spirit-filled life. You are undoubtedly a living definition exemplifying the word "helpmeet."

First Printing
January 2012

BAPTISM
Giving Depth to Baptismal Waters

List Price: **$13.75 each**
Plus postage and handling

Additional copies can be obtained from:

Disciple Maker Ministries

224 Fifth Avenue, N.W.
Hutchinson, MN 55350

612-750-5515

LanceKetchum@msn.com
www.disciplemakerministries.org

Quantity prices are available.

1.0

PREFACE BY DR. DAVID L. BROWN

Are Your Baptismal Waters Doctrinally Shallow? by Dr. Lance T. Ketchum is a MUST READ for every pastor, deacon, and should be read by every Christian. This book will provide a fuller understanding of the Bible's teaching on baptism, as well as explain the erroneous teachings surrounding this important biblical doctrine.

I have a number of books in my library on baptism. None of them covers the scope of Dr. Ketchum's book. This book gives the historical perspective of baptism, especially the timely chapter eight, "The Bloody Waters of Baptismal Persecution." Today, there is little discussion about the history of persecution accompanying biblical baptism by immersion! The book also carefully deals with the perversions, misunderstandings, misapplications, and misinterpretations that surround this important issue. One example is a clear explanation of the *Sacramental View of water baptism.* However, many Bible-believing Baptist churches have a *shallow* understanding of baptism as well. This book will deepen your understanding.

This book is also designed in such a way that is can easily be adapted to teach in a Sunday School class. Each chapter ends with discussion questions. In fact, I plan to use this book to teach on baptism in our Bible institute.

I have been a pastor for 40 years now. I must say, that I have profited reading this book. It will be worth your while to read it.

Dr. David L. Brown, Ph.D.
President of King James Bible Research Council
Senior Pastor of First Baptist Church of Oak Creek, WI

INTRODUCTION TO THESE STUDIES

Water baptism is a believer's testimonial declaration of his understanding of a covenantal commitment to God and to other members in a local church. Water baptism is a commitment regarding an understanding of a believer's responsibilities in his process of discipleship in being perfected "for the work of the ministry" (Ephesians 4:12). Therefore, water baptism connects the believer to a number of covenantal responsibilities.

1. Water baptism connects the believer to covenantal responsibilities know through the teaching of the Word of God by God's chosen and gifted pastors.

2. Water baptism connects the believer to covenantal responsibilities regarding formal membership in a local church. In this membership, each formal member becomes accountable to other formal members for his own individual spiritual growth and his own faithful to his commitment to Christ in water baptism.

3. Water baptism connects the believer to covenantal responsibilities in faithful attendance of all local church assemblies where that perfecting ministry in the discipleship process takes place.

4. Water baptism connects the believer to covenantal responsibilities of his own work in his discipleship through personal Bible study, extended reading, and devotional pursuit of the will of God for his life.

5. Water baptism connects the believer to covenantal responsibilities of the "work of the ministry" in personal evangelism through the proclamation of the Gospel of Jesus Christ. He accepts his responsibility to teach those whose are "born again" regarding the Lord's will in water baptism, uniting with a local church, and entering into the corporate responsibilities of a local church's outreach and discipleship ministries.

A professing believer that is never water baptized and who never formally unites with a local assembly of believers is foreign to the Scriptures of the New Testament. Therefore, we must conclude that anyone who professes to be a "born again" believer in Jesus Christ, who never submits to water baptism and who never formally unites with a local church, is living in disobedience to the biblical model of true Christianity.

TABLE OF CONTENTS

BAPTISM
Chapter One
Magic Water?

When a believer wants to understand a particular teaching of Scripture on any given subject or doctrine, he must begin with the Word of God (*Sola Scriptura – meaning the Bible alone*). We MUST insure that we do not come to the Scriptures with preconceived ideas (*presuppositions*) and then try to prove those preconceived ideas by finding Bible texts that prove those preconceived ideas. This method is known as *Proof Texting* and is the basic methodology of all Reformed Theology.

In most cases, Evangelical Christians are not prepared to deal with the theological problems that arise due to misunderstandings regarding the doctrines of water baptism and Holy Spirit baptism. The problems that come from misunderstanding what the Scriptures say about these doctrines are extremely serious because misunderstandings can result in misplaced faith and a false hope of having been "born again." In such cases, false beliefs regarding water baptism become "dead works" that must be repented of in order for true saving faith to exist (Hebrews 6:1-2).

"[37] Now when they heard *this {the idea is they heard, understood, and believed what was said}*, they were pricked in their heart *{they were under the conviction of their condemnation before God}*, and said unto Peter and to the rest of the apostles, Men *and* brethren, what shall we do *{to be saved}*? [38] Then Peter said unto them, Repent, and be baptized every one of you in the name of Jesus Christ <u>for</u> *{because of}* the remission of sins *{there is nowhere in the Word of God that remission of sins is affected by or the result of water baptism}*, and ye shall receive the gift of the Holy Ghost. [39] For the promise is unto you, and to your children, and to all that are afar off, *even* as many as the Lord our God shall call. [40] And with many other words did he testify and exhort, saying, Save yourselves from this untoward generation. [41] Then they that gladly received his word were baptized: and the same day there were added *unto them* about three thousand souls" (Acts 2:37-41).

There are two basic views on water baptism[1] within professing *Christianity,* using the word in the vaguest way possible. I say this because true *Christianity* is defined by how a person is biblically "born again" and how a person biblically lives his life as a priest before God. If the Bible's teaching on water baptism is perverted then the definition of *Christianity*, and *Christianity* itself, is perverted to that degree. Your view of water baptism will be determined by your understanding of the word "for" in Acts 2:38. The two main views are:

1. The sacramental view (Catholic and Reformed - with slight variations in the Reformed view) of water baptism, where the word "for" in Acts 2:38 means that water baptism is what *affects* or *causes* the "remission of sins" and by which one receives "the gift of the Holy Ghost" (i.e., baptismal regeneration).
2. The ordinance view of water baptism (*the cognitive view or typical view)* is where believing the Gospel and repentance of sin and "dead works" precedes water baptism *because* sin has been remitted. This happens *because* the "born again" believer has received "the gift of the Holy Ghost" *because* he has believed and repented. In this view, water baptism affects nothing. Water baptism is merely a way of *outwardly expressing* in a physical way our understanding of an *already accomplished spiritual reality.*

As we look at the composite of all Scripture references to water baptism (an *inductive methodology*) and formulate our understanding from what these texts say by themselves, apart from any presuppositions, we will clearly see that the *cognitive* view or *typical* view of water baptism is the only acceptable interpretation of God's intent in this ordinance. Where then do these presuppositions regarding the *Sacramental* view of water baptism come from? Simply put, they come from the pagan view of the *waters of regeneration* or *magic water.*

---

[1] Tenney, Merrill C., ed. *The Zondervan Pictoral Encyclopedia of the Bible, Vol. I.* Grand Rapids, MI :Zondervan Publishing House, (1982), pages 464-469

"The Greek philosophers believed water to be the original substance and that all things were made from it. The Koran states, 'From water we have made all things.'"[2]

Even many professing Christians and Theistic-evolutionists believe that this is what God is saying in Genesis 1:20. They misunderstand this verse to mean that the "waters" have regenerative powers. This is certainly NOT the intent of this verse.

"[20] And God said, Let the waters bring forth abundantly the moving creature that hath life, and fowl *that* may fly above the earth in the open firmament of heaven. [21] And God created great whales, and every living creature that moveth, which the waters brought forth abundantly, after their kind, and every winged fowl after his kind: and God saw that *it was* good. [22] And God blessed them, saying, Be fruitful, and multiply, and fill the waters in the seas, and let fowl multiply in the earth. [23] And the evening and the morning were the fifth day" (Genesis 1:20-23).

Two-thirds of the Earth's surface is covered by water. Genesis 1:20 gives us God's creative dictate for creatures living in the waters. The creatures of the seas were to "bring forth abundantly the moving creature that hath life." The creatures of the seas were intended to provide the vast majority of our meat resources just by nature of the way they are designed to reproduce in vast quantities.

"A Tench lay 1,000 eggs, a Carp 20,000, and Leuwenhoek counted in a middling sized Cod 9,384,000! Thus, according to the purpose of God, the waters bring forth abundantly. And what a merciful provision is this for the necessities of man! Many hundreds of thousands of the earth's inhabitants live for a great part of the year on fish only."[3]

Very early in man's religious corruption, ignorance began to cultivate ideas regarding procreation that soon developed into

[2]Orr, James. Gen. Ed. *International Standard Bible Encyclopedia 1939*, SwordSearcher Software 6.1
[3] Clarke, Adam. *Adam Clarke's Commentary on the Bible*. SwordSearcher Software 6.1

the early fertility cults of paganism. The ground began to be viewed as the *womb* of the *gods* and water came to be viewed as the *seed* of the *gods*. This all developed from the earliest form of what we know today as *scientific method* where *facts* are developed through the observation of physical phenomena. The observation was simple. When water came in contact with the ground through the heavy dew (it had never rained before the Great Flood), plants began to grow. The ground produced plants when the ground was watered. This was viewed to be the *magic of the gods*. It was believed that the ground had *magical properties* and water had *magical properties*.

Obviously, for those who believe in the Genesis account of creation, we understand that God has incorporated procreation as part of the laws of reproduction into Creation. Everything reproduced "after their kind" or "after his kind" (Genesis 1:21). Yes, earth and water are part of the ongoing process of procreation, but there is nothing *magical* in either. There are no *creative properties* within earth or water. This is a simple example of what happens when we take the knowledge of God as the Creator out of the *scientific process* – the result is *fairytales* like evolution and the evolution of thousands of religious fertility cults in varying forms of Pantheism. The theory of evolution is nothing more than another form of Pantheism.

"[20] For the invisible things of him from the creation of the world are clearly seen, being understood by the things that are made, *even* his eternal power and Godhead; so that they are without excuse: [21] Because that, when they knew God, they glorified *him* not as God, neither were thankful; but became vain in their imaginations, and their foolish heart was darkened. [22] Professing themselves to be wise, they became fools, [23] And changed the glory of the uncorruptible God into an image made like to corruptible man, and to birds, and fourfooted beasts, and creeping things" (Romans 1:20-23).

As these idolatrous and pagan cults of fertility evolved, they took the form of numerous idols representing the pagan gods that they believed controlled the *magic of fertility*. Various kinds of sacrificial systems were developed to appease, satisfy, or manipulate the pagan gods into releasing the *magic of fertility* through the rain and the flooding of the river plains such as the Nile in Egypt. These sacrificial practices became more bizarre and gory as they evolved. They developed into *blood lettings* in certain areas, animal sacrifices, and even human sacrifices – usually children and young virgins. All of these various rituals and sacrifices were to compel the pagan gods to release the *magic water* that had the power to regenerate. These various rituals were usually chronological with the cycles of the year and events were scheduled according to the movement of the Sun, Moon, planets, and stars. Astrology and numerous other cultic practices developed out of these cycles of the years.

> "Now, this doctrine of Baptismal Regeneration is essentially Babylonian. Some may perhaps stumble at the idea of regeneration at all having been known in the Pagan world; but if they only go to India, they will find, at this day, the bigoted Hindoos, who have never opened their ears to Christian instruction, as familiar with the term and the ideas as ourselves. The Brahmins make it their distinguishing boast, that they are 'twice-born' men, and that, as such, they are sure of eternal happiness.
>
> Now, the same was the case in Babylon, and there the new birth was conferred by baptism. In the Chaldean mysteries, before any instruction could be received, it was required, first of all, that the person to be initiated submit to baptism in token of blind and implicit obedience."[4]

Almost all of the pagan fertility cults worshipped the four elements (earth, water, wind, and fire) in some form because they viewed the four elements as physical expressions of the gods. The four elements were considered to be infused with the *divine essence* of a god or the gods.

> "Various forms of baptism, and the doctrine of baptismal regeneration, were common characteristics of pagan religion before the birth of Christ.
>
> The pagan water-worship cult is secondary only to sun-worship, in age and extent. Its native home was in the East, but it appears in all periods and on both hemispheres. It had two

---

[4] Hislop, Alexander. *The Two Babylons or The Papal Worship*. Neptune, N.J.: Loizeaux Brothers, Bible Truth Depot, (1858), 132.

phases: water as an object of worship, and as a means of inspiration; and water used in religious ceremonies to produce spiritual purity. These phases often mingle with each other.

This reverence for water, and faith in its cleansing efficacy, arose from the idea that it was permeated by the divine essence, from which it had supernatural power to enlighten and purify the soul, without regard to the spiritual state of the candidate. This doctrine of baptismal regeneration was transferred to Christianity before the close of the second century, and through it the Church was filled rapidly with baptized but unconverted pagans. Sun-worship and water-worship were closely united in the pagan *cultus,* as they were in the corrupted Christian baptism."[5]

Human fertility and reproduction especially were viewed through the cultish rituals of pagan fertility rites. Women went through elaborate rituals, drank magical potions, and recited various magical words over and over again in order to conceive children. Men had corresponding rituals and routines for their fertility rites. All of these fertility rituals and rites were believed to stimulate the regenerative powers of the gods that reside in the elements of earth, water, wind, and fire. Almost every pagan cult retains various aspects of these fertility cults, even the cults of *Christianity.* One aspect of the pagan fertility cults is that of *magic water* in the view of *baptismal regeneration* (although in the pagan cults, this *regeneration* was repeated often, usually yearly). Almost every pagan cult had some form of baptismal ritual, especially for infants. The pagan view of water baptism was that the water itself contained a *magical* cleansing efficacy.

There are literally hundreds of pagan *water-gods* throughout the world connected to various fertility rites and the properties of regeneration within the *sacred-waters.* Anyone with even a basic knowledge of paganism and idolatry knows this. None of the Roman Catholic or Reformed churches practices of infant baptism are even hinted at anywhere in the sacred Scriptures. These practices are adopted and adapted from ancient pagan worship as part of their fertility rites.

---

[5] Lewis, Abram Herbert - *Paganism Surviving in Christianity* . New York: G.P. Putnam's and Sons, (1892) 72-73
Note: Lewis is a Seventh Day Adventist and I would disagree with many of his false doctrines. However, his research on these ancient pagan religions is correct.

Although most of those who call themselves Evangelicals believe the Scriptures teach the *Ordinance View* of water baptism, they do not understand the difference in the way those who hold the *Sacramental View* of water baptism see salvation. Those who hold the *Ordinance View* of water baptism see salvation as an *event*. Those who hold the *Sacramental View* of water baptism see salvation as a *process*. For those holding the *Sacramental View* of water baptism, the ritual is merely initiatory into the lifelong *process* of salvation - affording the initiate the right to participate in, and benefit from, the efficacy of the other *sacraments*. Water baptism, in the *Sacramental View,* is a *step* in the *process* of salvation. We must remember that the *Sacramental View* of water baptism is a pagan and cultic view, not a Scriptural view.

Although Martin Luther is credited with being an *Evangelical* and teaching justification through faith, his faith was justification through faith in the *magic water* of baptism. Martin Luther was not an *Evangelical*. He taught the *Sacramental View* of salvation.

"In the second place, since we know now what Baptism is, and how it is to be regarded, we must also learn why and for what purpose it is instituted; that is, what it profits, gives and works. And this also we cannot discern better than from the words of Christ above quoted: He that believeth and is baptized shall be saved. Therefore state it most simply thus, that the power, work, profit, fruit, and end of Baptism is this, namely, to save. For no one is baptized in order that he may become a prince, but, as the words declare, that he be saved. But to be saved. we know. is nothing else than to be delivered from sin, death, and the devil, and to enter into the kingdom of Christ, and to live with Him forever.

Here you see again how highly and precious we should esteem Baptism, because in it we obtain such an unspeakable treasure, which also indicates sufficiently that it cannot be ordinary mere water. For mere water could not do such a thing, but the Word does it, and (as said above) the fact that the name of God is comprehended therein. But where the name of God is, there must be also life and salvation, that it may indeed be called a divine, blessed, fruitful, and gracious water; for by the Word such power is imparted to Baptism that it is a laver of regeneration, as St. Paul also calls it, Titus 3, 5.

But as our would-be wise, new spirits assert that faith alone saves, and that works and external things avail nothing, we answer: It is true, indeed, that nothing in us is of any avail but faith, as we shall hear still further. But these blind guides are unwilling to see this, namely, that faith must have something which it believes, that is, of which it takes hold, and upon which it stands and rests. Thus <u>faith clings to the water, and believes that it is Baptism, in which there is pure salvation and life</u>; not through the water (as we have sufficiently stated), but through the fact that it is embodied in the Word and institution of God, and the name of God inheres in it. Now, if I believe this, what else is it than believing in God as in Him who has given and <u>planted His Word into this ordinance</u>, and proposes to us this external thing wherein we may apprehend such a treasure?" (Underlining added)[6]

The proposition of the fact that there is efficacy in water baptism is a presupposition that has no biblical merit or foundation from any Bible text. The presupposition of the efficacy of the sacramental conference of salvific grace through water baptism is brought to numerous Bible texts and those texts are then interpreted through that presupposition.

---

[6] Luther, Martin. *The Large Catechism XIII Part Fourth of Baptism*-Translated by F. Bente and W.H.T. Dau, Published in: *Triglot Concordia: The Symbolical Books of the Ev. Lutheran Church.* St. Louis: Concordia Publishing House, 1921.
Note: available on www at:
http://www.iclnet.org/pub/resources/text/wittenberg/luther/catechism/web/cat-13.html

DISCUSSION QUESTIONS

1. Explain why *presuppositions* and *Proof Texting* generate misconceptions regarding what God's Word means.

2. List and explain the two basic views of water baptism.

3. Where does the *sacramental view* of water baptism originate?

4. Discuss why it is important to understand that there are no magical properties within either water or earth.

5. Discuss the influence of pagan fertility cults upon the sacramental view of water baptism.

6. Discuss why it is important to understand salvation as an *event* rather than a *process*.

7. Discuss Martin Luther's view of water baptism.

BAPTISM
Chapter Two
Magic Words and Infant Baptism

According to Martin Luther, we get the basic *formula* for making the waters of baptism efficacious when he says, "For mere water could not do such a thing, but the Word does it, and (as said above) the fact that the name of God is comprehended therein. But where the name of God is, there must be also life and salvation, <u>that it may indeed be called a divine, blessed, fruitful, and gracious water; for by the Word such power is imparted to Baptism that it is a laver of regeneration, as St. Paul also calls it, Titus 3, 5</u>." [7] This is important if we are going to understand the *Sacramental View* of infant baptism as well. When right words are said along with water baptism, the water's of baptism become "consecrated" waters "laden with supranatural power." We find this stated by Rudolph Bultmann as quoted by G.R. Beasley-Murray:

> "How are we to explain this attribution of saving grace to the performance of an outward act like baptism? One answer would take us back to primitive religion. Bultmann evidently so understands the position. Explaining the New Testament view he writes: 'the concept 'sacrament' rests upon the <u>assumption</u> that under certain conditions supranatural powers can be bound to natural objects of the world and to spoken words as their vehicles and mediators. If the conditions are fulfilled (if, for instance, the prescribed formula is correctly spoken and the material is thereby 'consecrated' – i.e. laden with supranatural power), and if the act is consummated according to the prescribed rite, then the supranatural powers go into effect, and the act, which apart from these conditions would be only a purely worldly, natural one like a bath or a meal, is itself a supranatural ceremony which works a miracle.' This reduces the baptism of the New Testament to the level of magic: by the correct recitation of the formula the water is laden with

---

[7] Ibid.

supranatural power, the pronouncement of the name brings the god on the scene and the miracle is performed."[8]

Again, as we see in this quote, we cannot understand the *Sacramental View* of water baptism apart from understanding the *assumptions* (presuppositions) imposed upon every Bible text where baptism is mentioned. There are also a number of other assumptions necessary to the *Sacramental View* of infant baptism.

"[25] And at midnight Paul and Silas prayed, and sang praises unto God: and the prisoners heard them. [26] And suddenly there was a great earthquake, so that the foundations of the prison were shaken: and immediately all the doors were opened, and every one's bands were loosed. [27] And the keeper of the prison awaking out of his sleep, and seeing the prison doors open, he drew out his sword, and would have killed himself, supposing that the prisoners had been fled. [28] But Paul cried with a loud voice, saying, Do thyself no harm: for we are all here. [29] Then he called for a light, and sprang in, and came trembling, and fell down before Paul and Silas, [30] And brought them out, and said, Sirs, what must I do to be saved? [31] And they said, Believe on the Lord Jesus Christ, and thou shalt be saved, and thy house. [32] And they spake unto him the word of the Lord, and to all that were in his house. [33] And he took them {*Paul and Silas*} the same hour of the night, and washed *their* stripes; and was baptized {*the jailer*}, he and all his, straightway. [34] And when he had brought them into his house, he set meat before them, and rejoiced, believing in God with all his house" (Acts 16:25-34).

I know of no one who holds to the *Sacramental View* of water baptism who does not admit that there is not one single reference to the baptism of infants in the Bible. Their teaching on infant baptism is based upon an *inference,* or an *assumption.* The presupposition is that water baptism saves. They then interpret the texts according to that presupposition. The assumption is twofold:

---

[8] Beasley-Murray, G.R. *Baptism in the New Testament.* Grand Rapids, MI: William B. Eerdmans Publishing Company, 264

16

1. There must have been infants in the Philippian jailer's "house."

2. Since all the people in the Philippian jailer's "house" were "baptized," the infants must also have been baptized.

They apply these assumptions to every *household* text. These primary household *proof texts* are as follows:

"[38] Then Peter said unto them, Repent, and be baptized every one of you in the name of Jesus Christ for the remission of sins, and ye shall receive the gift of the Holy Ghost. [39] For the promise is unto you, <u>and to your children</u>, and to all that are afar off, *even as many as the Lord our God shall call*" (Acts 2:38-39).

"[14] And a certain woman named Lydia, a seller of purple, of the city of Thyatira, which worshipped God, heard *us*: whose heart the Lord opened, that she attended unto the things which were spoken of Paul. [15] <u>And when she was baptized, and her household</u>, she besought *us*, saying, If ye have judged me to be faithful to the Lord, come into my house, and abide *there*. And she constrained us" (Acts 16:14-15).

"[14] I thank God that I baptized none of you, but Crispus and Gaius; [15] Lest any should say that I had baptized in mine own name. [16] And <u>I baptized also the household of Stephanas</u>: besides, I know not whether I baptized any other" (I Corinthians 1:14-16).

The *Sacramental View* of water baptism is an outgrowth of what is known as *Replacement Theology*. Those in *Replacement Theology* believe that the nation of Israel was replaced with a *State Church*. The Old Covenant *sacrifices* were replaced with New Covenant *sacraments*. Both the Old Covenant *sacrifices* and the New Covenant *sacraments* are viewed as efficacious to salvation. Old Covenant circumcision was replaced by New Covenant infant baptism. The Old Covenant priesthood was replaced with a New Covenant priesthood or clergy. All of these teachings are based upon presuppositions rather than biblical interpretation.

It is interesting that Paul refers to belief in the salvific efficacy of Old Covenant sacrifices as "works" and states emphatically that trust in such "works" for salvation does not save anyone. In fact, trust in such "works" (Ritualism or Moralism) condemns and is, in fact, a manifestation of unbelief (Hebrews 4:1-11). The epistle to the Hebrews addresses the problem raised by the Judaizers who were telling the Jewish Christians, that along with faith in Christ, they needed to keep the Jewish rituals, sacrifices, holy days, and the Temple rites in order to be saved. This is *grace plus works.* This was the corrupted view of Law keeping that the Judaizers sought to continue into Christianity.

"[1] Let us therefore fear, lest, a promise being left *us* of entering into his rest, any of you should seem to come short of it. [2] For unto us was the gospel preached, as well as unto them: but the word preached did not profit them, not being mixed with faith in them that heard *it*. [3] For we which have believed do enter into rest, as he said, As I have sworn in my wrath, if they shall enter into my rest: although the works were finished from the foundation of the world {*Revelation 13:8*}. [4] For he spake in a certain place of the seventh *day* on this wise, And God did rest the seventh day from all his works. [5] And in this *place* again, If they shall enter into my rest. [6] Seeing therefore it remaineth that some must enter therein, and they to whom it was first preached entered not in because of unbelief: [7] Again, he limiteth a certain day, saying in David, To day, after so long a time; as it is said, To day if ye will hear his voice, harden not your hearts. [8] For if Jesus {*should be Joshua*} had given them rest, then would he not afterward have spoken of another day. [9] There remaineth therefore a rest to the people of God. [10] For he that is entered into his rest {*through faith*}, he also hath ceased from his own works, as God *did* from his. [11] Let us labour therefore to enter into that rest, lest any man fall after the same example of unbelief" (Hebrews 4:1-11).

Paul refers to those teaching such things as the Judaizers taught were those that "trouble you" (Galatians 5:12). Even those of the Old Covenant who taught that the sacrifices of the Law were salvifically efficacious were condemned for such a contradiction against Christ.

"[1] Stand fast therefore in the liberty wherewith Christ hath made us free, and be not entangled again with the yoke of bondage. [2] Behold, I Paul say unto you, that if ye be circumcised, Christ shall profit you nothing. [3] For I testify again to every man that is circumcised, that he is a debtor to do the whole law. [4] Christ is become of no effect unto you, whosoever of you are justified by the law {*Moralism in keeping commandments or Ritualism in trusting in the sacrifices for remission of sins*}; ye are fallen from grace. [5] For we through the Spirit wait for the hope of righteousness by faith. [6] For in Jesus Christ neither circumcision availeth any thing, nor uncircumcision; but faith which worketh by love. [7] Ye did run well; who did hinder you that ye should not obey the truth? [8] This persuasion *cometh* not of him that calleth you. [9] A little leaven leaveneth the whole lump. [10] I have confidence in you through the Lord, that ye will be none otherwise minded: but he that troubleth you shall bear his judgment {*damnation for his false beliefs*}, whosoever he be. [11] And I, brethren, if I yet preach circumcision {*salvifically*}, why do I yet suffer persecution? then is the offence of the cross ceased. [12] I would they were even cut off {*amputated or taken away*} which trouble you" (Galatians 5:1-12).

The believer who understands the *Sacramental View* of water baptism understands that the person who believes this is NOT trusting in Christ's finished sacrifice. Faith in Christ has been misdirected to faith in water baptism. The *Sacramental View* of the New Covenant ordinance is no different from the efficacious view of the Old Covenant animal sacrifices. This view is condemned and rejected numerous times by Christ and the Apostles.

"[15] We *who are* Jews by nature, and not sinners of the Gentiles, [16] Knowing that <u>a man is not justified by the works of the law</u>, but by the faith of Jesus Christ, even we have believed in Jesus Christ, that we might be justified by the faith of Christ, and not by the works of the law: for by the works of the law shall no flesh be justified" (Galatians 2:15-16).

If circumcision, as part of the "works of the law," was replaced by infant baptism (and there is no such testimony anywhere in the Word of God), we see that the emphatic testimony of the inspired words of Scripture, as recorded by the Apostle Paul in Galatians 2:16, is that such "works" do not justify anyone before God.

"[1] For the law having a shadow of good things to come, *and* not the very image of the things, can never with those sacrifices which they offered year by year continually make the comers thereunto perfect. [2] For then would they not have ceased to be offered? because that the worshippers once purged should have had no more conscience of sins. [3] But in those *sacrifices there is* a remembrance again *made* of sins every year. [4] <u>For *it is* not possible that the blood of bulls and of goats should take away sins</u>. [5] Wherefore when he cometh into the world, he saith, Sacrifice and offering thou wouldest not, but a body hast thou prepared me: [6] In burnt offerings and *sacrifices* for sin thou hast had no pleasure" (Hebrews 10:1-6).

John Calvin gives us the classic *Sacramental View* of infant baptism that dominates Reformed Theology and Covenant (Replacement) Theology. Here again a presupposition dominates his reasoning. The presupposition is that children of covenant people, such as the Jews, were sealed by their circumcision into a *Covenant of Salvation.* For any reasonable person, this presupposition poses a considerable problem because only the male children of the Jews were circumcised. Does this then preclude Jewish girl children from the *Covenant of Salvation*?

"Now, if we are to investigate whether or not baptism is justly given to infants, will we not say that the man trifles, or rather is delirious, who would stop short at the element of water, and the external observance, and not allow his mind to rise to the spiritual mystery? If reason is listened to, it will undoubtedly appear that baptism is properly administered to infants as a thing due to them. The Lord did not anciently bestow circumcision upon them without making them partakers of all the things signified by circumcision. He would have deluded his people with mere imposture, had he quieted them with fallacious symbols: the very idea is shocking. He distinctly declares, that the circumcision of the infant will be instead of a seal of the promise of the covenant. But if the covenant remains firm and fixed, it is no less applicable to the children of Christians in the present day, than to the children of the Jews under the Old Testament. Now, if they are partakers of the thing signified, how can they be denied the sign? If they obtain the reality, how can

they be refused the figure? The external sign is so united in the sacrament <u>with the word</u>, that it cannot be separated from it: but if they can be separated, to which of the two shall we attach the greater value? Surely, when we see that the sign is subservient to the word, we shall say that it is subordinate, and assign it the inferior place. Since, then, the word of baptism is destined for infants, why should we deny them the sign, which is an appendage of the word? This one reason, could no other be furnished, would be amply sufficient to refute all gainsayers."[9]
(*The "gainsayers" that Calvin refers to are the Anabaptists.*)

It is necessary that we interject a biblical correction to the presupposition that the Jew entered into the Covenant of Abraham through circumcision. This is just not true. The Abrahamic Covenant was given in Genesis 12:1-3 in 1950 B.C. The Abrahamic Covenant was not instituted until thirty-seven years later (1921 B.C.) in Genesis chapter fifteen. There we are told "And he {*Abraham*} believed in the LORD; and he counted it to him for righteousness" (Genesis 15:6). Abraham was not circumcised until eleven years later in Genesis 17:24. Circumcision had nothing to do with the Abrahamic Covenant. One enters the Abrahamic Covenant by faith, not by circumcision or water baptism, infant or otherwise. Faith, totally apart from the "works of the law," is the common denominator for anyone to enter the Abrahamic Covenant.

"[6] Even as Abraham believed God, and it was accounted to him for righteousness. [7] Know ye therefore that they which are of faith, the same are the children of Abraham. [8] And the scripture, foreseeing that God would justify the heathen through faith, preached before the gospel unto Abraham, *saying*, In thee shall all nations be blessed. [9] So then they which be of faith are blessed with faithful Abraham. [10] For as many as are of the works of the law are under the curse: for it is written, Cursed *is* every one that continueth not in all things which are written in the book of the law to do them. [11] But that no man is justified by the law in the sight of God, *it is* evident: for, The just shall live by faith. [12] And the law is not of faith: but, The man that doeth them shall

---

[9] Calvin, John. *The Institutes of the Christian Religion*. translated by Henry Beveridge. Grand Rapids, MI: Christian Classics Ethereal Library, 1536. http://www.ccel.org/ccel/calvin/institutes.html, page 809 (accessed 2/7/2012).

live in them. [13] Christ hath redeemed us from the curse of the law, being made a curse for us: for it is written, Cursed *is* every one that hangeth on a tree: [14] That the blessing of Abraham might come on the Gentiles through Jesus Christ; that we might receive <u>the promise of the Spirit through faith</u>. [15] Brethren, I speak after the manner of men; Though *it be* but a man's covenant, yet *if it be* confirmed, no man disannulleth, or addeth thereto. [16] Now to Abraham and his seed were the promises made. He saith not, And to seeds, as of many; but as of one, And to thy seed, which is Christ. [17] And this I say, *that* the covenant {*of salvation 'by grace through faith'*}, that was confirmed before of God in Christ {*Genesis 3:15, 15:17; Revelation 13:8*}, <u>the law, which was four hundred and thirty years after</u>, cannot disannul, that it should make the promise of none effect. [18] For if the inheritance *be* of the law, *it is* no more of promise: but God gave *it* to Abraham by promise" (Galatians 3:6-18).

After all, Reformed Theology is reformed Roman Catholicism. The *Sacramental View* of infant baptism in Reformed Theology is a reformed view of Roman Catholic infant baptism. Common factors are the *consecration of the water* through saying the proper words invoking the Trinity and making the water *sacred*. The second common factor is that of *vicarious faith* on the part of the parents or godparents on behalf of the child. There are a number of aspects of Roman Catholic infant baptism excluded from the rite in Reformed churches.

"The rites that accompany the <u>baptismal ablution</u> are as ancient as they are beautiful. The writings of the early Fathers and the antique liturgies show that most of them are derived from Apostolic times.

The infant is brought to the door of the church by the sponsors {*new born infants are viewed as of the devil until baptized*}, where it is met by the priest. After the <u>godparents have asked faith from the Church of God in the child's name</u>, the priest breathes upon its face and exorcises the evil spirit. St. Augustine (Ep. cxciv, Ad Sixtum) makes use of this Apostolic practice of exorcising to prove the existence of original sin. Then the infant's forehead and breast are signed with the cross, the symbol of redemption.

Next follows the imposition of hands, a custom certainly as old as the Apostles. Some blessed salt is now placed in the mouth of the child. 'When salt', says the Catechism of the Council of Trent 'is put into the mouth of person to be baptized, it evidently imports that, by the doctrine of faith and the gift of grace, he should be delivered from the corruption of sin, experience a relish for good works, and be delighted with the food of divine wisdom.'

Placing his stole over the child the priest introduces it into the church, and on the way to the font the sponsors make a profession of faith for the infant. The priest now touches the ears and nostrils of the child with spittle. The symbolic meaning is thus explained (Cat. C. Trid.) 'His nostrils and ears are next touched with spittle and he is immediately sent to the baptismal font, that, as sight was restored to the blind man mentioned in the Gospel, whom the Lord, after having spread clay over his eyes, commanded to wash them in the waters of Siloe; so also he may understand that the efficacy of the sacred ablution is such as to bring light to the mind to discern heavenly truth.'

The catechumen now makes the triple renunciation of Satan, his works and his pomps, and he is anointed with the oil of catechumens on the breast and between the shoulders: 'On the breast, that by the gift of the Holy Ghost, he may cast off error and ignorance and may receive the true faith, 'for the just man liveth by faith' (Galatians 3:11); on the shoulders, that by the grace of the Holy Spirit, he may shake off negligence and torpor and engage in the performance of good works; 'faith without works is dead' (James 2:26)', says the Catechism.

The infant now, through its sponsors, makes a declaration of faith and asks for baptism. The priest, having meantime changed his violet stole for a white one, then administers the threefold ablution, making the sign of the cross three times with the stream of water he pours on the head of the child, saying at the same time: 'N___, I baptize thee in the name of the Father and of the Son and of the Holy Ghost.' The sponsors during the ablution either hold the child or at least touch it. If the baptism be given by immersion, the priest dips the back part of the head three times into the water in the form of a cross, pronouncing the sacramental words. The crown of the child's head is now anointed with chrism, 'to give him to understand that from that day he is united as a member to Christ, his head, and engrafted on His body; and therefore he is called a Christian from Christ, but Christ from chrism' (Catech.). A white veil is now put on the infant's head with the words: 'Receive this white garment, which mayest thou carry without stain before the judgment seat of Our Lord Jesus Christ, that thou mayest have eternal life. Amen.' Then a lighted candle is placed in the catechumen's hand, the priest saying: 'Receive this burning light, and keep thy baptism so as to be without blame. Observe the commandments of God; that, when Our Lord shall come to His nuptials, thou mayest meet Him together with all the Saints and mayest have life everlasting, and live for ever and ever. Amen.' The new Christian is then bidden to go in peace."[10] (underlining and items in { } added)

Alexander Hislop quotes from Prescott's book *Mexico*, volume III, pages 339-340 regarding Roman Catholic missionaries in Mexico. Prescott speaks regarding the practice of infant baptism among the pagan Indians. Remember, as you read this, what is being described is not the *infant baptism* as commonly practiced within paganized Christianity, but is part of the ancient rituals of pagan Sun worship. The Roman Catholic missionaries were astonished by the pagan practice that they saw being administered before their eyes because of the degree of similarity it had to their own ritual practices of infant baptism.

"When everything necessary for the baptism had been made ready, all the relations of the child were assembled, and the midwife, who was the person that performed the rite of baptism, was summoned. At early dawn, they met together in the court-yard of the house. When the sun had risen, the midwife, taking the child in her arms, called for a earthen vessel of water, while those about her placed the ornaments, which had been prepared for baptism, in the midst of the court. To perform the rite of baptism, she placed herself with her face toward the west, and immediately began to go through certain ceremonies . . . After this she sprinkled water on the head of the infant, saying, 'O my child, take and receive the water of the Lord of the world, which is our life, which is given for the increasing and renewing of our body. It is to wash and to purify. I pray that these heavenly drops may enter into your body and dwell there; that they may destroy and remove from you all the evil and sin which was given you before the beginning of the world, since all of us are

---

[10] Herbermann, C.G. Gen.Ed. *New Advent Catholic Encyclopedia.*, s.v. "Baptism: Ceremonies of Baptism" New York: Robert Appletonn Co., 1913. http://www.newadvent.org/cathen/02258b.htm (accessed 2/7/2012)

under its power . . .' She then washed the body of the child with water, and spoke in this manner: 'Whencesoever thou comest, thou that art hurtful to this child, leave him and depart from him, for he now liveth anew, and is born anew; now he is purified and cleansed afresh, and our mother Chalchivitlycue [the goddess of water] bringeth him into the world.' Having thus prayed, the midwife took the child in both hands, and, lifting him towards heaven, said, 'O Lord {*speaking to her form of the Sun god, Wodin*}, thou seest here thy creature, whom thou hast sent into the world, this place of sorrow, suffering, and penitence. Grant him, O Lord, thy gifts and inspiration, for thou art the great God, and with thee is the great goddess.'"[11] (text in { } added)

The presupposition of both adult and infant baptismal regeneration is that water baptism effects the baptism with the Holy Spirit. In other words, the baptism with the Holy Spirit results from and proceeds from water baptism. This presupposition can easily be rejected because this is not what we find in the evidence of Scripture testimonies.

---

[11] Hislop, Alexander, *The Two Babylons or The Papal Worship*. Neptune, N.J.: Loizeaux Brothers, Bible Truth Depot, page 133.

DISCUSSION QUESTIONS

1. Discuss Martin Luther's basic formula for making baptismal waters efficacious to salvation.

2. Explain what the author means when he states that those who teach infant baptism must understand that they must base what they teach (doctrine) upon *inference* or *assumption*.

3. Explain the *Sacramental View* of water baptism as the outgrowth of *Replacement Theology*.

4. Explain why a person trusting in the *Sacramental View* of water baptism is NOT trusting in Christ's finished redemption through His death, burial, and resurrection.

5. Define John Calvin's view of Sacramental water baptism and discuss why it fails to meet the biblical criterion.

6. Read Galatians 3:6-18. Was Abraham saved by his faith or by his circumcision? Why is this critical to understanding the false *presupposition* of *Replacement Theology*?

7. Discuss how the *Reformed Sacramental View* of water baptism is very similar to the *Roman Catholic Sacramental View* of water baptism.

BAPTISM
Chapter Three
Understanding Dispensation Transitions in the Acts of the Apostles

The question before us in dealing with the *Sacramental View* of water baptism is simple. Is the baptism with the Spirit effected (caused by or the result of) being water baptized, or is baptism with the Spirit effected by a biblical faith response to the finished redemptive work of Jesus Christ? Certainly, we can see a biblical pattern that it is faith that effects salvation, not water baptism. In other words, salvation is the outcome of repenting of sin and "dead works," understanding and believing the objective facts of the Gospel of Jesus Christ, confessing our belief that Jesus is Jehovah God incarnate, calling on the Name of Jesus to save us, and receiving the indwelling Holy Spirit of God as God's seal of our redemption. Baptism with water, the typical as representing cognizance of the actual baptism with the Holy Spirit, follows faith/believing and salvation.

"[26] And the angel of the Lord spake unto Philip, saying, Arise, and go toward the south unto the way that goeth down from Jerusalem unto Gaza, which is desert. [27] And he arose and went: and, behold, a man of Ethiopia, an eunuch of great authority under Candace queen of the Ethiopians, who had the charge of all her treasure, and had come to Jerusalem for to worship, [28] Was returning, and sitting in his chariot read Esaias the prophet. [29] Then the Spirit said unto Philip, Go near, and join thyself to this chariot. [30] And Philip ran thither to *him*, and heard him read the prophet Esaias, and said, Understandest thou what thou readest? [31] And he said, How can I, except some man should guide me? And he desired Philip that he would come up and sit with him. [32] The place of the scripture which he read was this, He was led as a sheep to the slaughter; and like a lamb dumb before his shearer, so opened he not his mouth: [33] In his humiliation his judgment was taken away: and who shall declare his generation? for his life is taken from the earth. [34] And the eunuch answered Philip, and said, I pray thee, of whom speaketh the prophet this? of himself, or of some other man? [35] Then Philip opened his mouth, and began at the same scripture, and preached unto him

Jesus. [36] And as they went on *their* way, they came unto a certain water: and the eunuch said, See, *here is* water; what doth hinder me to be baptized? [37] And Philip said, If thou believest with all thine heart, thou mayest. And he answered and said, I believe that Jesus Christ is the Son of God. [38] And he commanded the chariot to stand still: and they went down both into the water, both Philip and the eunuch; and he baptized him. [39] And when they were come up out of the water, the Spirit of the Lord caught away Philip, that the eunuch saw him no more: and he went on his way rejoicing" (Acts 8:26-39).

The biblical pattern in the order of salvation is that the indwelling of the Holy Spirit and the baptism with the Holy Spirit follows a faith decision. Due to misunderstanding of dispensational transitions between the Dispensation of the Law and the Dispensation of Grace (the Church Age), there are many who mistakenly see that the indwelling of the Spirit and the baptism with the Spirit take place at some undetermined time after salvation. These individuals believe that the baptism with the Spirit is a *second event* in a *process* of salvation (the *Full Gospel* view) or a second event in sanctification (the *Second Blessing* view).

"[3] Blessed *be* the God and Father of our Lord Jesus Christ, who hath blessed us with all spiritual blessings in heavenly *places* in Christ: [4] According as he hath chosen us in him before the foundation of the world, that we should be holy and without blame before him in love: [5] Having predestinated us unto the adoption of children by Jesus Christ to himself, according to the good pleasure of his will, [6] To the praise of the glory of his grace, wherein he hath made us accepted in the beloved. [7] In whom we have redemption through his blood, the forgiveness of sins, according to the riches of his grace; [8] Wherein he hath abounded toward us in all wisdom and prudence; [9] Having made known unto us the mystery of his will, according to his good pleasure which he hath purposed in himself: [10] That in the dispensation of the fulness of times he might gather together in one all things in Christ, both which are in heaven, and which are on earth; *even* in him: [11] In whom also we have obtained an inheritance, being predestinated according to the purpose of him who worketh all things after the counsel of his own will: [12] That we should be to the praise of his glory, who first trusted in Christ. [13] In whom ye also *trusted*, <u>after that ye heard the word of truth, the gospel of your salvation: in whom also after that ye believed, ye were sealed with that holy Spirit of promise,</u> [14] Which is the earnest of our inheritance until the redemption of the purchased possession, unto the praise of his glory" (Ephesians 1:3-14).

Undoubtedly, there would not be as many theological problems if those who believe Covenant Theology, Reformed Theology, and Pentecostal Theology understood the basics of Dispensationalism and dispensational transitions. It is because of their failure to understand Dispensationalism and dispensational transitions that they get so much distorted theology from the Acts of the Apostles. Within the Acts of the Apostles, we find a number of occasions where the baptism with the Holy Spirit happens to people already saved. This is because Old Covenant believers were not baptized with the Holy Spirit or indwelled by the Holy Spirit. We find this truth in Christ's promise of the Comforter in John chapter fourteen which answers the questions of the disciples regarding His departure after His crucifixion.

"[15] If ye love me, keep my commandments. [16] And I will pray the Father, and he shall give you another Comforter, that he may abide with you for ever; [17] *Even* the Spirit of truth; whom the world cannot receive, because it seeth him not, neither knoweth him: but ye know him; for he dwelleth with you {*prior to the Day of Pentecost*}, and shall be in you {*after the Day of Pentecost*}. [18] I will not leave you comfortless: I will come to you {*in the Person of the indwelling Holy Spirit*}. [19] Yet a little while, and the world seeth me no more; but ye see me: because I live, ye shall live also. [20] At that day {*the day of their indwelling*} ye shall know that I *am* in my Father, and ye in me, and I in you" (John 14:15-20).

The baptism with the Holy Spirit and the indwelling of the Holy Spirit are unique to New Covenant believers who believed that Jesus was the promised Messiah, that He accomplished complete propitiation of God for the sins of the world in His death on Calvary, and that He rose victorious over death in His resurrection. Old Covenant believers that were still alive after Pentecost, although they were saved in the Old Covenant sense of salvation, needed to believe in Jesus as

Messiah and the facts of the "finish" works of the Gospel. This did not change their salvation status, but they needed to confess Jesus as Lord, and call on the Name of Jesus to be transitioned into the New Covenant, by being baptized with the Holy Spirit, and receiving the indwelling of the Holy Spirit. Therefore, we have numerous instances of Scriptural evidences where this took place. One such example is Acts 19:1-6. This was unique only to the generation living at this time of dispensational transition. It is a grave error in biblical interpretation to see the baptism with the Holy Spirit and the indwelling of the Holy Spirit as following salvation or to be effected by water baptism as the norm. It is not! In fact, we have no Scriptural testimony to this after the Acts of the Apostles. The Acts of the Apostles covers the first twenty-seven years of Christianity (written in A.D. 60).

"[1] And it came to pass, that, while Apollos was at Corinth, Paul having passed through the upper coasts came to Ephesus: and finding certain disciples {*Old Covenant believers and disciples of John the Baptist*}, [2] He said unto them, Have ye received the Holy Ghost since ye believed? And they said unto him, We have not so much as heard whether there be any Holy Ghost. [3] And he said unto them, Unto what then were ye baptized? And they said, Unto John's baptism. [4] Then said Paul, John verily baptized with the baptism of repentance, saying unto the people, that they should believe on him which should come after him, that is, on Christ Jesus. [5] When they heard *this*, they were baptized in the name of the Lord Jesus {*by doing so, they identified themselves as disciples of Jesus*}. [6] And when Paul had laid *his* hands upon them, the Holy Ghost came on them {*this is the anointing of the Spirit, not the baptism with the Spirit*}; and they spake with tongues {*as a sign that the dispensational transition from Law to Grace had happened*}, and prophesied. [7] And all the men were about twelve" (Acts 19:1-6).

Speaking with other "tongues" (foreign languages) and the having the gift of prophesy were *signs* to the Jews of the coming of Messiah. In Acts 2:14-22, Peter says these *signs* were a fulfillment of the prophecy of Joel. Of course, these *signs* were only a temporary and partial fulfillment (*already, not yet*) until Christ establishes His Kingdom of earth and then these *sign gifts* will no longer be temporary.

"[28] And it shall come to pass afterward {*after the second coming of Christ and the establishment of the Kingdom Age*}, *that* I will pour out my spirit upon <u>all flesh</u> {*when the Kingdom Age begins, every person entering the Kingdom will be saved*}; and your sons and your daughters shall prophesy, your old men shall dream dreams, your young men shall see visions: [29] And also upon the servants and upon the handmaids in those days will I pour out my spirit. [30] And I will shew wonders in the heavens and in the earth, blood, and fire, and pillars of smoke. [31] The sun shall be turned into darkness, and the moon into blood, before the great and the terrible day of the LORD come {*vs. 30 and 31 refer to the seven year Tribulation on earth prior to the second coming*}. [32] And it shall come to pass, *that* whosoever shall call on the name of the LORD shall be delivered: for in mount Zion and in Jerusalem shall be deliverance, as the LORD hath said, and in the remnant whom the LORD shall call" (Joel 2:28-32).

Clearly, all of what is described in Joel 2:30-31 did not happen on the Day of Pentecost in Acts chapter two or at any other time recorded in the epistles of the New Testament. Portions of this prophecy were fulfilled and portions remain to be fulfilled. Even those portions of Joel's prophecy that were fulfilled were partially and temporarily fulfilled.

"[8] Charity never faileth: but whether *there be* prophecies, they shall fail; whether *there be* tongues, they shall cease; whether *there be* knowledge, it shall vanish away. [9] For we know in part, and we prophesy in part. [10] But when that which is perfect is come, then that which is in part shall be done away. [11] When I was a child, I spake as a child, I understood as a child, I thought as a child: but when I became a man, I put away childish things. [12] For now we see through a glass, darkly; but then face to face: now I know in part; but then shall I know even as also I am known. [13] And now abideth faith, hope, charity, these three; but the greatest of these *is* charity. (I Corinthians 13:8-13).

Why is it necessary to look at these details? It is necessary because these are all examples of dispensational transitional issues that do not continue into the Church Age.

Although water baptism always followed faith and salvation, after the dispensational transition that moved Old Covenant believers into the New Covenant, the baptism with the

Holy Spirit and indwelling of the Holy Spirit were synchronized with a faith decision to trust in Christ for salvation. Water baptism did not cause the baptism with the Spirit or the indwelling of the Spirit. This is the pattern we see in even John the Baptist's baptism of repentance. Did John's baptism *cause* repentance? Alternatively, was John's baptism something a person did to show that he had repented and was living with a changed view of sin and of God? Clearly, John the Baptist expected repentance to precede his baptism.

"⁷ But when he saw many of the Pharisees and Sadducees come to his baptism, he said unto them, O generation of vipers, who hath warned you to flee from the wrath to come? ⁸ Bring forth therefore fruits meet for repentance: ⁹ And think not to say within yourselves, We have Abraham to *our* father: for I say unto you, that God is able of these stones to raise up children unto Abraham. ¹⁰ And now also the axe is laid unto the root of the trees: therefore every tree which bringeth not forth good fruit is hewn down, and cast into the fire. ¹¹ I indeed baptize you with water unto repentance: but he that cometh after me is mightier than I, whose shoes I am not worthy to bear: he shall baptize you with the Holy Ghost, and *with* fire: ¹² Whose fan *is* in his hand, and he will throughly purge his floor, and gather his wheat into the garner; but he will burn up the chaff with unquenchable fire" (Matthew 3:7-12).

"³² And John bare record, saying, I saw the Spirit descending from heaven like a dove, and it abode upon him. ³³ And I knew him not: but he that sent me to baptize with water, the same said unto me, Upon whom thou shalt see the Spirit descending, and remaining on him, the same is he which baptizeth with the Holy Ghost. ³⁴ And I saw, and bare record that this is the Son of God" (John 1:32-34).

John the Baptist was the first in the New Testament to introduce the baptism with the Holy Spirit. The baptism with the Holy Spirit is unique to the Church Age dispensation (from the Day of Pentecost to the rapture). The baptism with the Holy Spirit was not available before the Cross or before the completion of the propitiatory work of Christ. We should not confuse the baptism with the Holy Spirit with anything the Holy Spirit of

God did in the Old Testament. John the Baptist is the messenger announcing the coming of the New Covenant in Jesus the Christ. Integral to that New Covenant is the baptism with the Holy Spirit. Therefore, understanding the baptism with the Holy Spirit defines God's working in the lives of His Redeemed. It is the finished work of Christ that opens the *dispensational door* for the baptism with the Holy Spirit. For instance, we know from Scripture that the baptism with the Spirit could not have happened before Jesus was glorified.

> "[37] In the last day, that great *day* of the feast, Jesus stood and cried, saying, If any man thirst, let him come unto me, and drink. [38] He that believeth on me, as the scripture hath said, out of his belly shall flow rivers of living water. [39] (But this spake he of the Spirit, which they that believe on him should receive: for the Holy Ghost was not yet *given*; <u>because</u> that Jesus was not yet glorified.)" (John 7:37-39).

The issue before us is answering the question, did the baptism of John the Baptist *cause* people to repent and be converted? Or, was the baptism of John the Baptist a means for people to express their conversion in turning from sin to faith in God? The confusion again comes from a poor translation of Mark 1:4, "John did baptize in the wilderness, and preach the baptism of repentance for the remission of sins." Did John's water baptism effect repentance and conversion or did John's baptism follow repentance and conversion? Robertson gives us the following comment on Mark 1:4:

> "**Unto remission of sins** (*eis aphesin hamartiôn*). This is a difficult phrase to translate accurately. Certainly John did not mean that the baptism was the means of obtaining the forgiveness of their sins or necessary to the remission of sins. The trouble lies in the use of *eis* which sometimes is used when purpose is expressed, but sometimes when there is no such idea as in Mt 10:41 and Mt 12:41. Probably 'with reference to' is as good a translation here as is possible. The baptism was on the basis of the repentance and confession of sin and, as Paul later explained (Ro 6:4), was a picture of the death to sin and resurrection to new life in Christ. This symbol was already in use by the Jews for proselytes who became Jews. John is

treating the Jewish nation as pagans who need to repent, to confess their sins, and to come back to the kingdom of God."[12]

Clearly, John the Baptist's water baptism did not effect, or cause, the repentance of the Jews, but rather was intended as a physical manifestation that repentance and conversion had already been accomplished "by grace through faith." John's baptism certainly could not have resulted in or caused *baptismal regeneration* since the Holy Spirit was not given in the sense of the baptism with the Holy Spirit and the indwelling of the Holy Spirit until *after* the Day of Pentecost. The Scriptures tell us that the Holy Spirit could not come in this new way until after Christ was ascended to the Father. Christ said this in John 16:7 and Peter said it in his message on the Day of Pentecost (Acts 2:31-33).

> "Nevertheless I tell you the truth; It is expedient for you that I go away: for <u>if I go not away, the Comforter will not come unto you</u>; but if I depart, I will send him unto you" (John 16:7).

> "[31] He seeing this before spake of the resurrection of Christ, that his soul was not left in hell, neither his flesh did see corruption. [32] This Jesus hath God raised up, whereof we all are witnesses. [33] <u>Therefore</u> {*logical and chronological procession*} being by the right hand of God exalted, and having received of the Father the promise of the Holy Ghost, <u>he hath shed forth this</u> {*the works of the promised Holy Spirit*}, which ye now see and hear" (Acts 2:31-33).

Although the finished work of Christ opened the *door* to the New Covenant (and closes the *door* to the Old), it is the baptism with the Holy Spirit that defines God's operations in everything Jesus does throughout the Church Age. Anyone ignorant of this one doctrine will be easily led astray, and many have been led astray. Therefore, it is important to take the time to establish what the Scriptures teach regarding this doctrine.

We must carefully avoid confusing the transitional period between the Old and New Covenants. At the time of

---

[12] Robertson, Archibald Thomas. *Word Pictures in the New Testament, Vol. I.* Grand Rapids, MI: Baker Book House, 253-254

the coming of the Holy Spirit at Pentecost, there were believers in both the Old Testament sense and the New Testament sense. The Old Testament believer was saved "by grace through faith" (as the common entrance into the promises of the Abrahamic Covenant, Galatians 3:16, 29) in what Messiah would do when He came. There were many saved Jews like this at the time of Christ's first advent. All of the disciples of John the Baptist (as well as John himself) were Old Testament *saints*. These Old Testament believers were saved, but were not baptized with the Holy Spirit.

In order to become New Covenant believers, these disciples of John the Baptist needed to recognize Jesus to be their promised Messiah, accept the work of the Cross as the fulfillment for which all that the Old Covenant rituals cried out (completeness), and publicly acknowledge (confess) their belief that Jesus was the incarnate Jehovah God who came to redeem them.

The baptism with the Spirit only happened to those who trusted in Jesus as the fulfillment of all Messianic prophecies of the Promised One. They no longer could just believe in the promised propitiation of God, but now need to understand and trust in the "finished" work (John 19:30). During this inter-testament period, Old Covenant believers became New Covenant believers by hearing the Gospel and accepting Jesus as the fulfillment of the Law. Apollos was a disciple of John the Baptist and was one such Old Covenant believer who became a New Covenant believer.

"[24] And a certain Jew named Apollos, born at Alexandria, an eloquent man, *and* mighty in the scriptures, came to Ephesus. [25] This man was instructed in the way of the Lord {*salvation 'by grace through faith'*}; and being fervent in the spirit, he spake and taught diligently the things of the Lord, knowing only the baptism of John. [26] And he began to speak boldly in the synagogue: whom when Aquila and Priscilla had heard, they took him unto *them*, and expounded unto him the way of God more perfectly. [27] And when he was disposed to pass into Achaia, the brethren wrote, exhorting the disciples to receive him: who, when he was come, helped them much which had believed through grace: [28] For he mightily convinced the Jews, *and that* publickly, shewing by the scriptures that Jesus was Christ" (Acts 18:24-28).

Another example of this is the household of Cornelius in Acts chapter ten. Cornelius, in all probability, was a proselyte of Judaism and a believer in the Old Covenant sense of "by grace through faith" in the Promised One. God sends a vision of an angel to Cornelius to tell him to go and find Simon Peter so that Peter could explain to him the "finished" work of Jesus the Messiah. Shortly thereafter, God gives a vision to Peter of the dispensational transition regarding the food laws of Israel and entering into the households of Gentiles (Acts 10:9-16). After Peter receives this vision and understands its meaning, he receives the Gentile Cornelius and teaches him about Jesus (Acts 10:17-33).

"[34] Then Peter opened *his* mouth, and said, Of a truth I perceive that God is no respecter of persons: [35] But in every nation he that feareth him, and worketh righteousness, is accepted with him. [36] The word which *God* sent unto the children of Israel, preaching peace by Jesus Christ: (he is Lord of all:) [37] That word, *I say*, ye know, which was published throughout all Judaea, and began from Galilee, after the baptism which John preached; [38] How God anointed Jesus of Nazareth with the Holy Ghost and with power: who went about doing good, and healing all that were oppressed of the devil; for God was with him. [39] And we are witnesses of all things which he did both in the land of the Jews, and in Jerusalem; whom they slew and hanged on a tree: [40] Him God raised up the third day, and shewed him openly; [41] Not to all the people, but unto witnesses chosen before of God, *even* to us, who did eat and drink with him after he rose from the dead. [42] And he commanded us to preach unto the people, and to testify that it is he which was ordained of God *to be* the Judge of quick and dead. [43] To him give all the prophets witness, that through his name whosoever believeth in him shall receive remission of sins. [44] While Peter yet spake these words, the Holy Ghost fell on all them which heard the word {*this is the anointed or filling of the Spirit*}. [45] And they of the circumcision which believed were astonished, as many as came with Peter, because that on the Gentiles also was poured out the gift of the Holy Ghost. [46] For they heard them speak with tongues, and magnify God. Then answered Peter, [47] Can any man forbid water, that these should not be baptized, which have received {*second aorist or past tense*} the Holy Ghost as well as we {*water baptism followed the baptism with and the indwelling of the Spirit*}? [48] And he commanded them to be baptized in the name of the Lord. Then prayed they him to tarry certain days" (Acts 10:34-48).

DISCUSSION QUESTIONS

1. Is baptism with the Spirit effected (caused by or the result of) being water baptized, or is baptism with the Spirit effected by a biblical faith response to the finished redemptive work of Jesus Christ?

2. Define the biblical pattern of the order of salvation. Discuss why understanding this is important.

3. Discuss why it is critical to understand Dispensational transitions in order to understand water baptism and Spirit baptism in the book of Acts.

4. Discuss Matthew 3:7-2 regarding the baptisms that John the Baptist administrated and why it is important to understand that God connects water baptism to practical sanctification and not to salvation.

5. Read John 7:37-39. From this text, explain why the baptism with the Holy Spirit could not have been available prior to the resurrection/glorification of Jesus.

6. How does understanding that there were Old Covenant believers needing to transition their faith in the Promised One to the Person of Jesus Christ help us understand the baptism with the Holy Spirit as a Dispensational transition from the Mosaic Covenant faith to New Covenant faith in the Messiah?

7. Explain Acts 10:17-33 from the context of your answer to question 6.

BAPTISM
Chapter Four
Translation Issues Regarding Baptism

The vast majority of what professing Christianity proclaims to be *baptism* is not biblical baptism at all. In fact, very few sects of *Christianity* (I use the term *Christianity* in the vaguest of sense of the word) actually *baptize*. The Greek word *baptizo* (bap-tid'-zo) means "to immerse, submerge" or at the least, "to make whelmed (i.e. fully wet)."[13] A contextual understanding of the practice that we call *baptism* today would actually translate *baptizo* as *immersion in water* or *burial in water*. This is the *only way* water baptism can fit the biblical model of practice. Therefore, it would be more accurate to say that most sects of *Christianity* do not *baptize*. They *sprinkle* and occasionally *pour*. Therefore, these sects do not only misrepresent the *purpose* of baptism, but also miss the *mode* of baptism as well.

> "[22] After these things came Jesus and his disciples into the land of Judaea; and there he tarried with them, and baptized {*baptizo*, bap-tid'-zo}. [23] And John also was baptizing in AEnon near to Salim, because there was much water there: and they came, and were baptized. [24] For John was not yet cast into prison. [25] Then there arose a question between *some* of John's disciples and the Jews about purifying. [26] And they came unto John, and said unto him, Rabbi, he that was with thee beyond Jordan, to whom thou barest witness, behold, the same baptizeth, and all *men* come to him. [27] John answered and said, A man can receive nothing, except it be given him from heaven. [28] Ye yourselves bear me witness, that I said, I am not the Christ, but that I am sent before him. [29] He that hath the bride is the bridegroom: but the friend of the bridegroom, which standeth and heareth him, rejoiceth greatly because of the bridegroom's voice: this my joy therefore is fulfilled. [30] He must increase, but I *must* decrease. [31] He that cometh from above is above all: he that is of the earth is earthly, and speaketh of the earth: he that cometh from heaven is above all. [32] And what he hath seen and heard, that he testifieth; and no man receiveth his testimony. [33] He that hath received his

---

[13] Strong, Augustus. *Strong's Greek Dictionary*. SwordSearcher Software 6.1

testimony hath set to his seal that God is true. [34] For he whom God hath sent speaketh the words of God: for God giveth not the Spirit by measure *unto him*. [35] The Father loveth the Son, and hath given all things into his hand. [36] He that believeth on the Son hath everlasting life: and he that believeth not the Son shall not see life; but the wrath of God abideth on him" (John 3:22-36).

Perhaps the first solution to the confusion being propagated by the word baptism is to stop using the transliteration of the Greek word *baptizo* and begin to actually translate it into English. The translation of *baptizo* would be the word *immerse* (in water). If we were to translate it according to its practical application, we would translate it as *bury* (in water). As we have already seen in the earlier studies, John the Baptist was undoubtedly immersing converts in water.

Almost all of the confusion of the purpose and mode of baptism is due to the centuries of theological condescension to the Anglican High Church men who translated the King James Version of the Bible into English. However, these men did not originate the transliteration of *baptizo* into the English *baptize*. The etymology of our English transliteration of *baptizo* into *baptize* most probably comes from the Old French in the early 1300's.

"c. 1300, *bapteme*, from O.Fr. *batesme*, *bapteme* (11c., Mod.Fr. *bapteme*), from L. *baptismus*, from Gk. *baptismos*, noun of action from *baptizein*"[14]

John Wycliffe used this transliteration in his English translation (known as Wycliffe's Bible) in AD 1382. Wycliffe translated from the Latin Vulgate into English. Below is John Wycliffe's translation of John 3:22-23:

"[22] Aftir these thingis Jhesus cam, and hise disciplis, in to the loond of Judee, and there he dwellide with hem, and baptiside. [23] And Joon was baptisinge in Ennon, bisidis Salym, for many

---

[14] Harper, Douglas. *Online Etymology Dictionary* http://www.etymonline.com/index.php?allowed_in_frame=0&search=baptism &searchmode=none (accessed: 2/7/2012).

watris weren there; and thei camen, and weren baptisid" (John 3:22-23).[15]

There is no apparent reason for John Wycliffe to transliterate either the Greek *baptizo* or the Latin *baptismus,* since Wycliffe was undoubtedly a Lollard[16]. The Lollards, like the Anabaptists, rejected infant baptism[17] (*Padeobaptism*) for *Credobaptism[18]* and they baptized by immersion. Even in the Church of England (the Anglican Church), it is generally agreed that sprinkling infants did not begin until AD 1644.[19] Therefore, it would be incorrect to assume the translators of the King James Bible purposely transliterated the Greek *baptizo* into the English *baptize* because they did not believe in immersion. The King James Bible was translated in AD 1611, thirty-three years before *infant sprinkling* was adopted.

Martin Luther created a German translation of the Bible from "Erasmus's second edition (1519) of the Greek New Testament, known as the Textus Receptus,"[20] first printed in AD 1534. Luther translated the Greek word *baptizo* into the German word *taufte* and *taufen*.[21] Both forms of the word mean to immerse. Although Luther believed in remission of sins through the consecrated waters of baptism ("the laver of regeneration"), he undoubtedly believed that immersion was the only acceptable mode of baptism. (In using words from different languages regarding *baptism*, it is like saying, "immersion is the only acceptable mode of immersion.") Luther's belief in both *baptismal regeneration* and in immersion as the only acceptable mode is clear in his sermon from AD 1518:

"First baptism is called Greek *baptismos*, in Latin *mersio*, that is,

---

[15] Wycliffe, John. *Wycliffe's Translation* (SwordSearcher Software 6.1)
[16] Christian, John T., *A History of the Baptists Together with Some Account of Their Principles and Practices -Vol. 1*. Texarkana: Bogard Press 1992, 186.
[17] Ibid., page 186.
[18] Ibid., page 187.
[19] Ibid. page 173.
[20] http://en.wikipedia.org/wiki/Luther_Bible (accessed: 2/7/2012)
[21] Bible Data Base: http://www.bibledbdata.org/onlinebibles/german_l/43_003.htm (accessed: 2/7/2012)

when we dip anything wholly in water, that it is completely covered over. And although in many provinces it is no longer the custom (in other provinces it was the custom) to thrust the children into the font and to dip them; but they only pour water with the hands out of the font; nevertheless, it should be thus, and would be right, that after speaking aloud the word (baptize) the child or any one who is to be baptized, be completely sunk down into the water, and dipt again and drawn out, for without doubt in the German tongue the word (*taufe*) comes from the word *tief* (deep), that a man sinks deep into the water, what he dips. That also the signification of baptism demands, for it signifies that the old man and sinful birth from the flesh and blood shall be completely drowned through the grace of God. Therefore, a man should sufficiently perform the signification and a right perfect sign. The sign rests in this, that a man plunge a person in water in the name of the Father, etc., but does not leave him therein but lifts him out again; therefore it is called being lifted out of the font or depths. And so must all of both these things be the sign; the dipping and the lifting out. Thirdly, the signification is a saving death of the sins and of the resurrection of the grace of God. The baptism is a bath of the new birth. Also a drowning of the sins in the baptism (Opera Lutheri, I. 319. Folio edition)."[22]

Luther's statements here reflect the conflicting and convoluted discussions of the Reformers who were trying to reconcile the arguments of Roman Catholicism that they rejected and the theological arguments of Augustine who they respected. That tension continues in almost all Reformed circles today.

Williams Tyndale (c. AD 1484 – 1536) translated what came to be known as the Tyndale Bible (the New Testament) in AD 1526. Tyndale was greatly influenced by Luther, but his theology was more like Wycliffe. Some even purported that he was a Baptist. Tyndale followed Wycliffe in transliterating the Greek *baptizo* into the English *baptize*. Most probably, the intent in this transliteration is not to cloud the issue of the mode of Baptism because, like Wycliffe, Tyndale was very vocal about immersion being the accepted mode. Most probably, the intent is noble by using the transliteration to bring more focus upon the

---

[22] Christian, John T. *A History of the Baptists Together with Some Account of Their Principles and Practices -Vol. I*. Texarkana: Bogard Press 1992, 108.

meaning of the ordinance than merely upon the *mode*. Tyndale's Bible "is credited with being the first English translation to work directly from Hebrew and Greek texts."[23] His translation of John 3:22-23 is as follows:

> "[22] After these thinges cam Iesus and his disciples into the Iewes londe and ther he haunted with them and baptised. [23] And Iohn also baptised in Enon besydes Salim because ther was moche water there and they came and were baptized" (John 3:22-23).

Tyndale wrote extensively and most of his writings are summarized in a book published as ***The Works of William Tyndale***. Christian gives us a number of quotes from that work.

> "Davis (History of the Welsh Baptist, 21) claims that William Tyndale (A.D. 1484-1536) was a Baptist. . . 'Llewellyn Tyndale and Hezekiah Tyndale were members of the Baptist church at Abergaverney, South Wales.'. . It is certain he shared many views held by the Baptists; but that he was a member of a Baptist church is nowhere proved. He always translated the word *ecclesia* by the word congregation, and held to a local conception of a church (Tyndale, Works II. 13. London, 1831). There were only two offices in the church, pastor and deacons (I. 400). The elders or bishops should be married men (I. 265). Upon the subject of baptism he is very full. He is confident that baptism does not wash away sin. 'It is impossible,' says he, 'that the waters of the river should wash out hearts' (Ibid. 30). Baptism was a plunging into the water (Ibid. 287). Baptism to avail must include repentance, faith and confession (III. 179). The church must, therefore, consist of believers (Ibid. 25). His book in a wonderful manner states accurately the position of the Baptists."[24]

The Geneva Bible (New Testament published in AD 1557 and the complete Bible published in AD 1560) was the first English translation widely accepted by Reformed churches. Its marginal references and comments were very *Calvinistic*. The

---

[23] http://en.wikipedia.org/wiki/Tyndale_Bible (accessed: 2/7/2012)
[24] Christian, John T. *A History of the Baptists Together with Some Account of Their Principles and Practices -Vol. I*. Texarkana: Bogard Press, 1992, 187-188.

43

Geneva Bible was translated from the *Textus Receptus* by William Whittingham (c. 1524-1579).[25] He was a stout Calvinist and was married to John Calvin's sister.[26] The Geneva Bible also transliterates the Greek *baptizo* into the English *baptize*. The Geneva Bible translates John 3:21-22 as follows:

"[22] After these things, came Iesus & his disciples into the lande of Iudea, and there taried with them, and baptized. [23] And Iohn also baptized in Enon besides Salim, because there was much water there: and they came, and were baptized" (John 3:21-22).[27]

Although John Calvin believed that baptism was dipping or immersing someone in water, he argued against it for practical reasons – most churches were not near lakes or rivers. After all, we should be clear about this – the Baptist's argument for re-baptizing people was not because they had been improperly immersed when they were baptized. The Baptist's argument for re-baptizing people was because these people were not saved when they were baptized by immersion. There is no record of adult or infant baptism (except in Roman Catholicism) by anything other than immersion until Calvin came on the scene. The Church of England did not begin sprinkling infants until about AD 1644 (33 years after the King James Version of AD 1611).

Calvin's influence upon theology and the practices implemented into churches by rationalism should not be underestimated. His Soteriological, Eschatology, Pneumatology, and especially his Ecclesiology were all a horrible mess.

"The influence of John Calvin had begun to be felt in English affairs. His books had appeared in translations in England. He was responsible in a large measure for the demon of hate and fierce hostility which the Baptists of England had to encounter. He advised that 'Anabaptists and reactionists should be alike put to death' (Froude, History of England, V. 99). . . 'These altogether deserve to be well punished by the sword, seeing that they do conspire against God, who had set him in his royal seat'

[25] http://en.wikipedia.org/wiki/William_Whittingham (accessed 2/7/2012)
[26] Ibid.
[27] *The Geneva Bible*. SwordSearcher Software 6.1

(referring to the Lord Protector Somerset of the Church of England)."[28] Statement in ( ) added.

"There are two examples in the writings of John Calvin which go to show that the Baptists were in the practice of dipping. Calvin came in direct contact with the Baptists and well knew their opinions, for he married the widow of a Baptist preacher. In the first example, he defines a well-known passage the meaning of the word. He says: 'The word signifies to immerse, and it is certain that the rite of immersion was observed in the ancient church (Calvin, Institutes, Bk.IV. c 15).'
Immediately following this statement he makes a reply to a Baptist who urged that Acts 19:3-5 taught rebaptism. Calvin says to the Baptist: 'That if ignorance vitiated the former baptism, so that another baptism is made to correct it; they were the first of all to be baptized by the apostles, who in all the three years after their baptism scarcely tasted a small particle of the measure of the sincere doctrine. Even now among us, where would there be sufficient rivers for a repetition of the dipping of so many, who in ignorance of the compassion of the Lord, are daily corrected among us (Ibid, c. 15. Sec. 18).'"[29]

Clearly, Calvin believed that immersion was the biblical mode and meaning of the word *baptizo*. He simply thought that requiring enough water to immerse everyone being baptized was just too impractical (the *argument of inconvenience*). The real motivating factor for Calvin's rejection of immersion as the only acceptable mode of baptism, as ridiculous as it seems, is apparent. Calvin hated the Baptists and wanted them all eliminated by simply having them executed.

The Geneva Bible and The Bishop's Bible were motivated by the desire to counteract the *Free Church Movement* (also later known as the *Separatist Movement*) that was greatly advanced by the publication of the Tyndale Bible. Luther and Calvin continued the Theonomic view of the Church following Augustine's Preterist view of Eschatology. The word PRETERIST comes from the Latin word PRAETER, meaning

---

[28] Christian, John T. *A History of the Baptists Together with Some Account of Their Principles and Practices -Vol. I.* Texarkana: Bogard Press, 1992, 198-199.
[29] Ibid., 112-113.

PAST or BEYOND. This view holds that John's prophecies regarding the end-times referred to events of his own day, about AD 90. In this view, the Church was already in the Kingdom Age (the one-thousand year time span was later allegorized away from a literal one-thousand years). The Church in this view was both a governing force ruling both secularly and spiritually as a *State Church*. This is what Calvin established in Geneva, Luther in Germany, and the Church of England in England and Scotland. Catholicism was the *State Church* almost everywhere else in Europe. A primary issue of the Reformation was the separation of these various sects of Reformed churches from the *State Church* of Roman Catholicism.

However, in almost every case, these new sects simply established their own reformed *State Churches*. The erroneous Ecclesiology of most of the Reformers did not change much. In the midst of this were the Baptists, Presbyterians, Free Church of Scotland, Anglican Separatists, and Free Lutherans who altogether rejected the idea of a *State Church* and opposed it through preaching, teaching, and writings. Tyndale was correct in his view of the Church as consisting only in local congregations and a separation of these churches from State interference.

The Geneva Bible was filled with marginal notes of Calvinism. The Free Presbyterians used the Geneva Bible because of Calvin's doctrines of election and predestination. The high churchmen of the Church of England developed the Bishops Bible (first published in AD 1568 and revised in AD 1572, also called the Great Bible because of its huge size) to be used in the Church of England to counteract the Free Presbyterian view of church government (the view that each local church was governed by a group of elected "lay elders"[30]). The translation of John 3:21-22 from the Bishops Bible is below and follows the precedent of Wycliffe in transliterating the Greek *baptizo* into the English *baptize*.

"[22] After these thynges, came Iesus and his disciples into the lande of Iurie, and there he taryed with the, & baptized. [23] And Iohn also baptized in Enon, besides Salim, because there was much water there: and they came, and were baptized" (John 3:21-22).

The influence of the rationalism of Calvinism was a transitional issue in systematic theology. There was an influence of rationalism in the development of *Sacramental View* of sprinkling in infant baptism as opposed to the *Ordinance View* of Baptists by immersion. Calvin's Reformed Systematic Theology was reformed Augustinianism, which was Roman Catholic Systematic Theology. However, Calvin continued using Augustine's deductive methodology (known as *Aristotelian Syllogism*). Without going into too much depth, Calvin's Soteriology is based upon one major presupposition – only certain people are chosen by God to be saved. These are called "the elect." From that *wrong* presupposition, the rest of Calvin's theology *logically* proceeds. Although Calvin rejected baptismal regeneration, infant baptism was the first step in the process of salvation of the "elect" (the *Ordo Salutis*). They believed that through infant baptism, the infant was baptized into the "body of Christ" (the State Church), which caused the infant to be *in Christ*. For them, there was no salvation apart from being part of the Church.

> "But as it is now our purpose to discourse of the visible Church, let us learn, from her single title of Mother, how useful, nay, how necessary the knowledge of her is, since there is no other means of entering into life unless she conceive us in the womb and give us birth, unless she nourish us at her breasts, and, in short, keep us under her charge and government, until, divested of mortal flesh, we become like the angels (Mt. 22:30)."[31]

Calvin's discussions on baptism are so conflicted and convoluted that it often appears he is arguing with himself. It is amazing that those fascinated with Calvin's theology do not see the numerous contradictions between his statements rejecting regeneration through water baptism and some degree of efficacy in the sacrament.

---

[31] Calvin, John. *The Institutes of the Christian Religion.* Public Domain: Christian Classics Ethereal Library.
http://www.ccel.org/ccel/calvin/institutes.html (accessed 2/7/2012).

"Then, again, when they {*the Anabaptists*} ask us what faith for several years followed our baptism, that they may thereby prove that our baptism was in vain, since it is not sanctified unless the word of the promise is received with faith, our answer is, that being blind and unbelieving, we for a long time did not hold the promise which was given us in baptism, but that still the promise, as it was of God, always remained fixed, and firm, and true. Although all men should be false and perfidious, yet God ceases not to be true (Rom. 3:3, 4); though all were lost, Christ remains safe. We acknowledge, therefore, that at that time baptism profited us nothing, since in us the offered promise, without which baptism is nothing, lay neglected. Now, when by the grace of God we begin to repent, we accuse our blindness and hardness of heart in having been so long ungrateful for his great goodness. But we do not believe that the promise itself has vanished, we rather reflect thus: God in baptism promises the remission of sins, and will undoubtedly perform what he has promised to all believers. That promise was offered to us in baptism, let us therefore embrace it in faith. In regard to us, indeed, it was long buried on account of unbelief; now, therefore, let us with faith receive it. Wherefore, when the Lord invites the Jewish people to repentance, he gives no injunction concerning another circumcision, though (as we have said) they were circumcised by a wicked and sacrilegious hand, and had long lived in the same impiety. All he urges is conversion of heart. For how much soever the covenant might have been violated by them, the symbol of the covenant always remained, according to the appointment of the Lord, firm and inviolable. Solely, therefore, on the condition of repentance, were they restored to the covenant which God had once made with them in circumcision, though this which they had received at the hand of a covenant-breaking priest, they had themselves as much as in them lay polluted and extinguished."[32] (Words in { } added)

Calvin's view of infant baptism *sealed* the infant into the "Covenant" (the view that the *State Church* replaces National Israel as the benefactors of the Abrahamic Covenant). He therefore *logically* equates infant baptism with circumcision and

---

[32] Calvin, John. *The Institutes of Religion*. Book Fourth. Public Domain: Christian Classics Ethereal Library, 802.
http://www.ccel.org/ccel/calvin/institutes.html (accessed 2/7/2012).

logically replaces circumcision with infant baptism. It has already been shown unequivocally that no one, including Abraham, entered the Abrahamic Covenant through circumcision. Infant circumcision was a physical sign of identification with national Israel and a reminder of the responsibility of the "blessing and curse" of the Mosaic Covenant. National Israel was a composite of Jews saved by faith, like Abraham, and individual Jews who had not understood the *Gospel in the Law*. Nonetheless, the Mosaic Covenant was made with national Israel and the "blessing and curse" of the Mosaic Covenant would come to national Israel according to their faithfulness in keeping – enforcing or adjudicating the "statutes and judgments" *as a nation*. The promise of the Mosaic Covenant, of which circumcision is a *sign* and a *seal*, is therefore "blessing" when obedient and "curse" (chastisement) when disobedient. The promise of the Mosaic Covenant was NOT salvation. Infant circumcision never assured that any child would be saved. Yet this is how Calvin *logically* equates infant circumcision with infant baptism.

"Now, if we are to investigate whether or not baptism is justly given to infants, will we not say that the man trifles, or rather is delirious, who would stop short at the element of water, and the external observance, and not allow his mind to rise to the spiritual mystery? If reason is listened to, it will undoubtedly appear that baptism is properly administered to infants as a thing due to them. The Lord did not anciently bestow circumcision upon them without making them partakers of all the things signified by circumcision. He would have deluded his people with mere imposture, had he quieted them with fallacious symbols: the very idea is shocking. He distinctly declares, that the circumcision of the infant will be instead of <u>a seal of the promise of the covenant</u>. But if the covenant remains firm and fixed, it is no less applicable to the children of Christians in the present day, than to the children of the Jews under the Old Testament. Now, if they are partakers of the thing signified, how can they be denied the sign? If they obtain the reality, how can they be refused the figure? The external sign is so united in the sacrament with the word, that it cannot be separated from it: but if they can be separated, to which of the two shall we attach the greater value? Surely, when we see that the sign is subservient to the word, we shall say that it is subordinate, and assign it the inferior place. Since, then, the word of baptism is destined for infants, why should we deny them the sign, which is an appendage of the word? This one reason, could no other be furnished, would be amply sufficient to refute all gainsayers. The objection, that there was a fixed day for circumcision, is a mere quibble. We admit that we are not now, like the Jews, tied down to certain days; but when the Lord declares, that though he prescribes no day, yet he is pleased that infants shall be formally admitted to his covenant, what more do we ask?"[33]

A far as Calvin was concerned, the mode of baptism, whether by immersion in water, pouring on of water, or the sprinkling of water was of no consequence to his *Sacramental View*. Calvin gave that permission to Reformed churches based on logic. Once a logical argument was found to support both infant baptisms by sprinkling, then the search for *proof texts* to support the presuppositional argument began.

"Whether the person baptised is to be wholly immersed, and that whether once or thrice, or whether he is only to be sprinkled with water, is not of the least consequence: churches should be at liberty to adopt either, according to the diversity of climates, although it is evident that the term *baptise* means to immerse, and that this was the form used by the primitive Church."[34]

In this statement, Calvin seeks to justify two practices that existed within Roman Catholicism that he wanted to continue.

1. Infant Baptism
2. Sprinkling or pouring as the mode of baptism

Although Calvin understood and stated that "it is evident that the term *baptise* means to immerse, and that this was the form used by the primitive Church," he sought to justify a departure from that practice in the sprinkling of infants. He did so on the basis of a logical argument derived from a perverted

---

[33] Calvin, John. *The Institutes of the Christian Religion.* Book fourth, chapter 16, paragraph 5, 809-810.
[34] Ibid., Book fourth, chapter 15, paragraph 19, 804.

view of *Sola Scriptura*. There were two basic theological positions of *Sola Scriptura* coming out of the Reformation. One said, *whatever the Bible does not disallow, we allow*. The other said, *whatever the Bible confirms, we confirm*. Neither position was immune from the imposition of presuppositions and proof-texting. Those coming out of Roman Catholicism were especially prone to two other faulty methodologies - the *imposition of presuppositions* and *proof-texting*. Calvin's argument was that the Scriptures did not *disallow* infant baptism by sprinkling and therefore infant baptism by sprinkling should be *allowed* (the *argument of silence*).

Calvin hated the Baptists and certainly did not want to become a Baptist. Infant baptism was the place where Calvin drew his *line in the sand* for his so-called *Reformation* of Roman Catholicism. He understood that if he could not defend the practice of infant baptism by sprinkling, by condescending he would admit of necessity that the Baptists were justified in rejecting the infant sprinklings of new converts and the necessity of re-baptizing these people after they confessed Christ. The Baptists did not view this as a *re-baptism* since infant sprinkling was never a real baptism in the first place. Since Calvin had been supporting the persecution and killing of Baptist for years because the Baptists rejected infant sprinkling as a baptism, he could not cross that line without condemning himself for his own barbaric injustices against them. Ulrich Zwingli (AD 1484 – 1531) in Switzerland, a contemporary of Calvin, came to this same point of departure in his reformation of Roman Catholicism. Zwingli was unwilling to cross this line. He also persecuted and had Baptists murdered. This is a common pattern among Reformed theologians of this time-period.

DISCUSSION QUESTIONS

1. What is the Greek word in the Bible that is translated "baptize"? Define this word and discuss why the vast majority of what people call baptisms are not baptisms at all.

2. Who was apparently the first man to transliterate the Greek word *baptizo* into a new English word *baptize*?

3. Discuss some reason why this transliteration was a good idea.

4. Discuss why we can know that this transliteration was not allowing for infant sprinkling.

5. How did Luther's German translation of the Bible translate the Greek word *baptizo*? Discuss why this important.

6. John Calvin believed that baptism in the Bible was dipping or immersing. Discuss why he justified sprinkling and why his view of the purpose of water baptism affects his justification for sprinkling.

7. How did Calvin's attitude towards the Baptists affect his view of water baptism?

BAPTISM
Chapter Five
The Metaphorical Use of "Wash" in Baptism

It is well established from an inductive evaluation of all Bible texts regarding water baptism that water has no cleansing capabilities when it comes to sin. Any person with a basic understanding of Scripture ought to plainly understand the metaphorical use of physical washing in water. People fail to understand metaphors, similes, and types because authoritarian spiritual leaders have exchanged the reality of what these literary tools are intended to portray by making them the reality.

Judaism did this with the Sabbath Day, the Holy Days like Passover, the various sacrifices, and the ritual washings. Liturgical Christianity does the same with various false views of Sabbatarianism, Holy Days such as Lent, and by making water baptism and the Lord's Supper into *sacraments* through which a participant receives the grace of God. Liturgical Christianity, like apostate Judaism, replaces the spiritual reality with the type, thereby making the typical efficacious. This is the purest form of Legalism and is, in fact, what defines Legalism in varying degrees of its existence.

The book of Hebrews gives us thirteen chapters of inspired Scriptures detailing the superiority of the realities of the New Covenant over the shadows or types of the Old Covenant (the Mosaic Covenant). We can never understand the metaphorical use of words like "wash" and "sprinkled" unless we understand them from their use in their Old Covenant types. As we see these metaphorical terms used in transitioning from the Old Covenant to the New Covenant, we must also see that the typical is realized in the actual. The Old Covenant ritual washings *typified* the cleansing of sin for sanctification, not salvation. This was equally true of the references to "sprinkling." Sanctification is always the context of baptisms in the Old Covenant. Salvation is never in view.

"[1] Now of the things which we have spoken *this is* the sum: We have such an high priest, who is set on the right hand of the throne of the Majesty in the heavens; [2] A minister of the sanctuary, and of the true tabernacle, which the Lord pitched, and not man. [3] For every high priest is ordained to offer gifts and sacrifices: wherefore *it is* of necessity that this man have somewhat also to offer. [4] For if he were on earth, he should not be a priest, seeing that there are priests that offer gifts according to the law: [5] <u>Who serve unto the example and shadow of heavenly things</u>, as Moses was admonished of God when he was about to make the tabernacle: for, See, saith he, <u>*that* thou make all things according to the pattern shewed to thee in the mount</u>" (Hebrews 8:1-5).

A text that is often very confusing for many Christians is the statement in Acts 22:16 - "And now why tarriest thou? arise, and be baptized, and wash away thy sins, calling on the name of the Lord." This lays in the context where the Apostle Paul is giving the testimony of his salvation and his calling to be an Apostle of the Lord Jesus Christ. Rather than offering confusion, the statement actually provides clarification for God's intent in water baptism. Just like in the Old Covenant, ritual washings were connected with purification or sanctification for service. Old Covenant baptisms were NEVER connected with salvation.

The account of Paul's testimony in Acts chapter twenty-two involves his testimony of salvation AND his consecration as an Apostle of Jesus Christ. It is important to understand that this event took place in Jerusalem. Paul spoke in Hebrew to Jews (Acts 21:40). Unless we understand the *Jewishness* of the emphasis of Paul's testimony to these Jews, we will miss the significance of the distinctions within his testimony.

"[1] Men, brethren, and fathers, hear ye my defence *which I make* now unto you. [2] (And when they heard that he spake in the Hebrew tongue to them {*signifying that he was not a Hellenized Jew*}, they kept the more silence {*they listened to him speak in Hebrew because this gave him immediate credibility*}: and he saith,) [3] I am verily a man *which am* a Jew, born in Tarsus, *a city* in Cilicia, yet brought up in this city at the feet of Gamaliel {*one of the most prominent celebrated doctors of Jewish Law giving greater credibility to Paul's education*}, *and* taught according to the perfect manner of the law of the fathers, and was zealous toward God, as ye all are this day. [4] And I persecuted this way {*the Christian way; John 14:6*} unto the death, binding and

54

delivering into prisons both men and women {*Christians or followers of Christ; 'the way'*}. [5] As also the high priest doth bear me witness, and all the estate of the elders {*the Sanhedrin*}: from whom also I received letters unto the brethren, and went to Damascus, to bring them which were there bound unto Jerusalem, for to be punished {*his commission from the Sanhedrin to act in this official capacity*}. [6] And it came to pass, that, as I made my journey, and was come nigh unto Damascus about noon, suddenly there shone from heaven a great light round about me. [7] And I fell unto the ground, and heard a voice saying unto me, Saul, Saul, why persecutest thou me? [8] And I answered, Who art thou, Lord? And he said unto me, I am Jesus of Nazareth, whom thou persecutest. [9] And they that were with me saw indeed the light, and were afraid; but they heard not the voice of him that spake to me. [10] And I said, What shall I do, Lord {*believing and acknowledging Jesus to be 'Lord'*}? And the Lord said unto me, Arise, and go into Damascus; and there it shall be told thee of all things which are appointed for thee to do {*his calling as an Apostle*}. [11] And when I could not see for the glory of that light, being led by the hand of them that were with me, I came into Damascus. [12] And one Ananias, a devout man according to the law, having a good report of all the Jews which dwelt *there*, [13] Came unto me, and stood, and said unto me, Brother {*now already saved*} Saul, receive thy sight. And the same hour I looked up upon him. [14] And he said, The God of our fathers hath chosen thee, that thou shouldest know his will, and see that Just One, and shouldest hear the voice of his mouth {*qualifying Paul to be Apostle*}. [15] For thou shalt be his witness unto all men of what thou hast seen and heard. [16] And now why tarriest thou? arise, and be baptized {*consecration to his Apostleship*}, and wash away thy sins {*the typical ritual purgation of the Old Covenant involved in consecration*}, calling on the name of the Lord {*invoking the Name of the Lord*}. [17] And it came to pass, that, when I was come again to Jerusalem, even while I prayed in the temple, I was in a trance; [18] And saw him {*Jesus*} saying unto me, Make haste, and get thee quickly out of Jerusalem: for they {*the Jews that Paul was previously connected with in the persecution of the Christians*} will not receive thy testimony concerning me. [19] And I said, Lord, they {*the Jewish Christians*} know that I imprisoned and beat in every synagogue them that believed on thee: [20] And when the blood of thy martyr Stephen was shed, I also was standing by, and consenting unto his death, and kept the raiment of them that slew him. [21] And he said unto me, Depart: for I will send thee far hence unto the Gentiles" (Acts 22:1-21).

The significance of the baptism mentioned in Acts 22:16 is the common thread that runs throughout Scripture. It identifies the already saved believer with an understanding of both positional sanctification "in Christ" and the need for practical sanctification to serve Christ.

"[9] Know ye not that the unrighteous shall not inherit the kingdom of God? Be not deceived: neither fornicators, nor idolaters, nor adulterers, nor effeminate, nor abusers of themselves with mankind, [10] Nor thieves, nor covetous, nor drunkards, nor revilers, nor extortioners, shall inherit the kingdom of God. [11] And such were some of you: but ye are washed {*aorist, middle, indicative*}, but ye are sanctified {*aorist, passive, indicative*}, but ye are justified {*aorist, passive, indicative*} in the name of the Lord Jesus, and by the Spirit of our God" (I Corinthians 6:9-11).

The use of the middle voice in the phrase "ye are washed" is significant to our understanding of this as a reference to water baptism. Robertson gives us considerable insight into this significance:

"**But ye were washed** (*apelousasthe*). First aorist middle indicative, not passive, of *apolouô*. Either direct middle, ye washed yourselves, or indirect middle, as in Ac 22:16, ye washed your sins away (force of *apo*). This was their own voluntary act in baptism which was the outward expression of the previous act of God in cleansing (*hêgiasthête*, ye were sanctified or cleansed before the baptism) and justified (*edikaiôthête*, ye were put right with God before the act of baptism)."[35]

There are three commonly promoted significances regarding water baptism. We should understand each of them and then determine which of the three finds biblical support in practice.

---

[35] Robertson, Archibald Thomas. *Word Pictures in the New Testament, Vol. 4* Grand Rapids: Baker Book House, 1930, 120.

1. Baptism is a cleansing of sin or a washing away of the sin of the soul.

2. Baptism is a confession of faith in Christ upon which God acts, regenerating the sinner. In this view, water baptism is the *means* of confessing faith in Christ through which we are "born again." (Baptism is not found in Romans 10:1-13.)

3. Baptism is a commitment to become a disciple of Jesus, involving death to a life of sin and a commitment to live a new life of righteousness in the resurrection power of the indwelling Christ. In this view, water baptism is the time of an individual's acknowledgment of his vocational calling as a priest and his need of practical sanctification. This practical sanctification must be a reality before God can consecrate (empower) him for the "work of the ministry." Therefore, water baptism is a beginning point of a moment-by-moment focus and emphasis in a believer's life. Certainly, this is the biblical model we see repeated in Scripture and this is the model that should be repeated in the emphasis of water baptism practiced throughout the Church Age.

The command to baptize was intimately, intricately, and inseparably connected to Christ's command to preach the Gospel to all nations in generating a continuum of disciples through all generations until Jesus returns. Only saved people were baptized. A baptized disciple who continually fails to be involved in *evangelism* (soul winning, leading the saved to be baptized into a local church to be discipled, and living the teachings of Jesus) manifests an individual whose baptism was nothing more than *getting wet*. Either that individual did not understand the significance of water baptism, or his commitment in water baptism was a lie. Salvation is the *entrance level* of our Father/child relationship with God. Privileges and responsibilities come with the intimacy of any relationship. To claim the privileges of intimacy without accepting the responsibilities of intimacy is an abuse of the relationship and manifests the nonexistence of intimacy. Water baptism is the *entrance level* of our relationship with Jesus as His disciple. To claim to be a disciple of Jesus without death to the "old man" and a daily commitment to faithfulness to Christ is like saying your wedding vows to your wife while all along you know your mistress is waiting for you outside the church.

In the Old Testament, "washings" (referred to in Hebrews 9:10 using the Greek word *baptismos*) were ritual purgations that were typical of spiritual cleansing. Nowhere in the Old Testament is there any indication that these ritual "washings" were able actually to wash away sin. The very notion of such nonsense is to miss the typology of the Old Covenant rituals and sacrifices in order to make efficacious those rituals and sacrifices. They were not. The notion that Old Covenant "washings" were able to actually cleanse away sin is nothing but a silly idea that the *Magic Water* paganists continue to propagate. Yet, the apostate priesthood of Israel misled the people to believe that the commandments, the sacrifices, and the rituals were the means to their righteousness before God and means to their salvation. None of the "works of the law" had any merit outside of faith in the Promised Seed of Genesis 3:15 in the Protevangelium and in the Abrahamic Covenant (Galatians 3:16). Justification (the imputation of God's righteousness) through faith in the Promised Seed ALWAYS preceded the issues of Law-keeping. God gave the commandments, the sacrifices, and the rituals *for saved* people. None of the commandments, the sacrifices, and the rituals were given *to save* someone. This ought to be obvious to anyone who has read Isaiah, the Gospels, the epistle to the Romans, the epistle to the Hebrews, or the epistle to the Galatians.

Since it is obvious that the commandments, the sacrifices, and the rituals could not save anyone, why would we think that they could sanctify anyone? Ritual "washings" merely portrayed the necessity for spiritual cleanness before the Lord. We can be confident that God is concerned about our external cleanliness (see Leviticus chapter fifteen) for health reasons and for the benefit of those around us, but this is not the spiritual significance of ritual "washings." The Old Covenant "washing" were intent upon manifesting the need for spiritual cleanliness before the sacrifices could be acceptable to God. This was portrayed in a very simplistic manner of which we all can identify. We want the cook to wash his hands BEFORE he prepares our food. Every farm wife wants her husband to take off his barn boots

BEFORE he comes into her kitchen.

"[17] And the LORD spake unto Moses, saying, [18] Thou shalt also make a laver *of* brass, and his foot *also of* brass, to wash *withal*: and thou shalt put it between the tabernacle of the congregation and the altar, and thou shalt put water therein. [19] For Aaron and his sons shall wash their hands and their feet thereat: [20] When they go into the tabernacle of the congregation, they shall wash with water, that they die not; or when they come near to the altar to minister, to burn offering made by fire unto the LORD: [21] So they shall wash their hands and their feet, that they die not: and it shall be a statute for ever to them, *even* to him and to his seed throughout their generations" (Exodus 30:17-21).

The point of washing their hands and feet before preparing the meat for the sacrifices is to prevent the transfer of uncleanness from them to the sacrifices. Science did not understand the infectious nature of microbes until the mid to late 1800's. The most dangerous place to give birth was in a hospital where 20% to 50% of mothers were being infected and dying because of the unwashed hands of the doctors delivering their babies. During the Civil War, thousands of wounded soldiers died, not because of their wounds, but because of the unwashed hands of field medics and doctors who passed on Staph infection and Gangrene from one patient to the next. The Creator understood the infectious nature of "uncleanness" long before humanity ever discovered it. Yet the necessity of the priests to wash their hands and feet before ministering in the Tabernacle was only typical of the infectious nature of spiritual "uncleanness." It was not long before the typical picture lost its connection to the spiritual reality therein portrayed.

"[10] In the four and twentieth *day* of the ninth *month*, in the second year of Darius, came the word of the LORD by Haggai the prophet, saying, [11] Thus saith the LORD of hosts; Ask now the priests *concerning* the law, saying, [12] **If one bear holy flesh in the skirt of his garment, and with his skirt do touch bread, or pottage, or wine, or oil, or any meat, shall it be holy?** And the priests answered and said, **No** {*holiness could not be transferred from something holy to something unholy*}. [13] Then said Haggai, **If *one that is* unclean by a dead body touch any**

of these, shall it be unclean? And the priests answered and said, **It shall be unclean** {*uncleanness or defilement contaminated everything it came in contact with*}. [14] Then answered Haggai, and said, So *is* this people, and so *is* this nation before me, saith the LORD; and so *is* every work of their hands; and that which they offer there *is* unclean {*because the priesthood had failed to maintain their holiness/separation before the Lord and had defiled themselves and their ministry*}. [15] And now, I pray you, consider from this day and upward, from before a stone was laid upon a stone in the temple of the LORD: [16] Since those *days* were, when *one* came to an heap of twenty *measures*, there were *but* ten {*chastisement rather than blessing*}: when *one* came to the pressfat for to draw out fifty *vessels* out of the press, there were *but* twenty {*chastisement rather than blessing*}. [17] I smote you with blasting and with mildew and with hail in all the labours of your hands {*chastisement rather than blessing*}; yet ye *turned* not to me {*refused to repent*}, saith the LORD. [18] Consider now from this day and upward, from the four and twentieth day of the ninth *month, even* from the day that the foundation of the LORD'S temple was laid, consider *it*. [19] Is the seed yet in the barn? yea, as yet the vine, and the fig tree, and the pomegranate, and the olive tree, hath not brought forth {*the potential for blessing or chastisement was still open*}: from this day {*the decision regarding your repentance right now*} will I bless *you*" (Haggai 2:10-19).

Water baptism connects the believer to his understanding of this spiritual dynamic of the absolute necessity of separation from a life of sin and worldliness. Water baptism also connects him to separation unto God through "the work of the ministry" in a lifetime of evangelism and discipleship. Although physical cleanliness is important, healthy, and will certainly affect whether or not someone will want to be near you long enough for you to explain the Gospel and lead him to Christ, *spiritual cleanness* is the essential to God's supernatural enablement and blessing upon your "work of the ministry." This was Christ's emphasis to the "scribes and Pharisees" in their accusation against the disciples for eating bread with unwashed hands.

"[1] Then came to Jesus scribes and Pharisees, which were of Jerusalem, saying, [2] Why do thy disciples transgress the tradition of the elders? for they wash not their hands when they eat bread.

³ But he answered and said unto them, Why do ye also transgress the commandment of God by your tradition? ⁴ For God commanded, saying, Honour thy father and mother: and, He that curseth father or mother, let him die the death. ⁵ But ye say, Whosoever shall say to *his* father or *his* mother, *It is* a gift, by whatsoever thou mightest be profited by me; ⁶ And honour not his father or his mother, *he shall be free.* Thus have ye made the commandment of God of none effect by your tradition. ⁷ *Ye* hypocrites, well did Esaias prophesy of you, saying, ⁸ This people draweth nigh unto me with their mouth, and honoureth me with *their* lips; but their heart is far from me. ⁹ But in vain they do worship me, teaching *for* doctrines the commandments of men" (Matthew 15:1-9).

Believers quickly and easily slip into externalism and lose the spiritual significance of ordinances. This is certainly true with water baptism. How important is it to God that believers are sensitive to the sin in our lives? How important is it that believers understand that sin (any sin) is a great offense against the holy character of our heavenly Father? Does God merely want us to recognize the fact that we are sinners and that sin is therefore inevitable in our lives? God's Word clearly teaches that He expects His children to both recognize what sin is and turn from that sin in our lives. God wants us to hate sin as He hates sin. God wants us to have a broken heart about the sin in our lives. Water baptism is intended to be a moment in time when we testify to our accountability peers in a local church that we understand this spiritual reality and that we are making a lifetime commitment to live it.

Have you ever found yourself saying, "Sure, I did that but what do you expect? After all, we are all sinners?" How easy it is to justify our failures before the grace and mercy of a forgiving God. How easy it is to justify our rebellion and refusal to obey God's commands. How easy it is to justify our refusal to do the work He has called us to do. How easy it is to take His grace and mercy for granted.

The central theme of the book of Zechariah (as well as Haggai and Malachi) is that the children of Israel were expected to live exemplary lives of holiness before a world of people who were very hostile to the absolute truths of God's Word.

Regardless of how morally and politically wicked the world was toward God's children, they were to *maintain* a relationship of personal holiness with God and before the world. That relationship involved maintaining sensitivity towards sin while the world around them was becoming completely insensitive to sin.

Believers were responsible to *maintain* a Biblical perspective of who they were as a people – God's children. Their first and foremost responsibility was to live in such a way as to please God and bring Him glory (as models of the *Christ-life*), regardless of how peculiar that lifestyle appeared to the world.

Christians cannot seem to grasp the difference between the completeness of our salvation "in Christ" positionally and our daily responsibilities of the momentary (*moment-by moment*) repentance of sin and cleansing of sin to maintain our practical sanctification before the Lord. Without this *moment-by-moment* maintenance of our intimacy with God in "fellowship," we quickly lapse into deadly externalism, spiritual pretense, and ritual *God-stuff* without the intimacy of our relationship with God. This is one of the spiritual truths Jesus taught His disciples by washing their feet.

"[1] Now before the feast of the passover, when Jesus knew that his hour was come that he should depart out of this world unto the Father, having loved his own which were in the world, he loved them unto the end. [2] <u>And supper being ended</u> {*after the Lamb was killed, the blood applied, and the flesh eaten*}, the devil having now put into the heart of Judas Iscariot, Simon's *son*, to betray him; [3] Jesus knowing that the Father had given all things into his hands, and that he was come from God, and went to God; [4] He riseth from supper, and laid aside his garments; and took a towel, and girded himself. [5] After that he poureth water into a bason, and began to wash the disciples' feet, and to wipe *them* with the towel wherewith he was girded. [6] Then cometh he to Simon Peter: and Peter saith unto him, Lord, dost thou wash my feet? [7] Jesus answered and said unto him, What I do thou knowest not now; but thou shalt know hereafter. [8] Peter saith unto him, Thou shalt never wash my feet. Jesus answered him, <u>If I wash thee not, thou hast no part with me</u>. [9] Simon Peter saith unto him, Lord, not my feet only, but also *my* hands and *my* head {*ignorance often speaks the loudest and its demands are foolish*}. [10] Jesus saith to him, He that is washed needeth not save to wash *his* feet, but is clean every whit: and ye are clean {*alluding to justification 'by grace through faith'*}, but not all. [11] For he knew who should betray him; therefore said he, Ye are not all clean. [12] So after he had washed their feet, and had taken his garments, and was set down again, he said unto them, Know ye what I have done to you? [13] Ye call me Master and Lord: and ye say well; for *so* I am. [14] If I then, *your* Lord and Master, have washed your feet; ye also ought to wash one another's feet {*mutuality in the local church in helping to maintain one another's sanctification*}. [15] For I have given you an example, that ye should do as I have done to you. [16] Verily, verily, I say unto you, The servant is not greater than his lord; neither he that is sent greater than he that sent him. [17] If ye know these things, happy {*blessed of God*} are ye if ye do them" (John 13:1-17).

Obviously, Jesus washing the feet of His disciples was intended to typify that they would be contaminated daily by their contact with the world. They would occasionally and regularly fail, falter, and fall. They would need to be regularly and habitually cleansed. It should be equally obvious that no one believed that *foot washing* was to be a continued ordinance in the church (at least we never see it practiced anywhere else in Scripture). Equally obvious was the fact that no one understood this to mean that sanctification came through regularly washing your feet in water.

DISCUSSION QUESTIONS

1. Discuss how authoritarian spiritual leaders misuse and twist biblical metaphors and similes.

2. Discuss why the epistle to the Hebrews is an important document to correct abuses of metaphors and similes as they portray biblical types.

3. Read and explain Acts 22:1-21 regarding the *Jewishness* of Paul's explanation of water baptism in its relationship to practical sanctification rather than to salvation.

4. Explain the importance of understanding the use of the *middle voice* in Acts 22:16 in the statement, "but ye were washed."

5. List and discuss the three most commonly prompted significances of water baptism.

6. Since water baptism connects a believer to practical sanctification rather than salvation, what is its connecting purpose to that believer's responsibilities of evangelism? Discuss why a baptized believer who fails to try to evangelize his acquaintances is an anomaly to true Christianity.

7. Discuss how God intends water baptism to connect the saved person to his daily responsibilities as a Christian.

Chapter Six
Understanding Our Threefold Salvation

Another point of confusion regarding baptism is that many people fail to see the word "save" in the Bible in the context of its use in the threefold sense of salvation. The word "save" does not always refer to being saved from Hell. There are three aspects of salvation in the Word of God (I Thessalonians 5:23-24). The believer must understand these three aspects of salvation and determine to which aspect of salvation the context of a Bible text is referring. The three aspects of salvation are:

1. Salvation of the believing sinner's *soul* from Hell "by grace through faith" – this aspect of salvation is positionally complete "in Christ" (Colossians 2:10-15).
2. Salvation of the believer's *life* (or *spirit*) through practical sanctification – this aspect of salvation is a supernatural working of the Holy Spirit throughout the believer's life (Romans 8:9-11; I Thessalonians 5:23-24).
3. Salvation of the believer's *body* through glorification (Romans 8:28-30; II Thessalonians 2:13).

These three aspects of salvation are all positionally complete the moment we respond in faith to the message of the Gospel of Jesus Christ. The Scofield Reference Bible gives us an extensive note on the trichotomy of man in I Thessalonians 5:23. The theological significance of the trichotomy of man in our understanding of various Bible texts is critical to the proper interpretation of those texts as these texts relate to the three aspects of a believer's salvation.

"Man a *trinity*. That the human soul and spirit are not identical is proved by the facts that they are divisible. Heb 4:12 and that soul and spirit are sharply distinguished in the burial and resurrection of the body. It is sown a natural body (soma psuchikon= 'soul-body'), it is raised a spiritual body (soma pneumatikon). 1Co 15:44. To assert, therefore, that there is no difference between soul and spirit is to assert that there is no difference between the mortal body and the resurrection body. In Scripture use, the distinction between spirit and soul may be traced. Briefly, that distinction is that the spirit is that part of man which 'knows' 1Co 2:11 his mind; the soul is the seat of the affections, desires, and so of the emotions, and of the active will, the self. 'My soul is exceeding sorrowful' Mt 26:38 see also Mt 11:29; Joh 12:27. The word transliterated 'soul' in the O.T. (nephesh) is the exact equivalent of the N.T. word for soul (Gr. psuche), and the use of 'soul' in the O.T. is identical with the use of that word in the N.T. (see, e.g.) De 6:5; 14:26; 1Sa 18:1; 20:4,17; Job 7:11; 14:22; Ps 42:6; 84:2. The N.T. word for spirit (pneuma) like the O.T. (ruach), is trans. 'air', 'breath', 'wind,' but predominantly 'spirit,' whether of God (e.g.) Ge 1:2; Mt 3:16 or of man Ge 41:8; 1Co 5:5. Because man is 'spirit' he is capable of God-consciousness, and of communication with God Job 32:8; Ps 18:28; Pr 20:27 because he is 'soul' he has self- consciousness Ps 13:2; 42:5-6,11 because he is 'body' he has, through his senses, world consciousness."[36]

Failure in determining to which aspect of salvation a particular Bible text refers can cause great confusion. This is certainly true of the statement in I Peter 3:20-21. As we read this text, we must ask ourselves a few simple questions. Was Noah and his family already saved from eternal condemnation prior to their entering into the ark? Is the text referring to the salvation of their souls from Hell or the salvation of their lives from drowning in the floodwaters?

"[8] But Noah found grace in the eyes of the LORD. [9] These *are* the generations of Noah: <u>Noah was a just man</u> *and* perfect in his generations, *and* Noah walked with God. [10] And Noah begat three sons, Shem, Ham, and Japheth" (Genesis 6:8-10).

The statement that "Noah was a just man" is not referring to Noah's own personal righteousness giving him merit with God. This statement refers to Noah's justification by God "by grace through faith. God clarifies this in Hebrews chapter eleven. The *Pulpit Commentary* gives us this clarification of the text:

"[B]etter 'justified' or declared righteous, being derived from the

---

[36] *1917 Scofield Reference Bible Notes*. SwordSearcher Software 6.1

Piel form of the verb (Furst). 'Evidently the righteousness here meant is that which represents him as justified in view of the judgment of the Flood, by reason of his faith, [Heb 11:7] (Lange).'"[37]

"By faith Noah, being warned of God of things not seen as yet, moved with fear, prepared an ark to the saving of his house; by the which he condemned the world, and became heir of the righteousness which is by faith" (Hebrews 11:7).

The phrase "prepared an ark to the saving of his house" refers to the salvation of Noah's family. Although it was the work or action of preparing the ark that saved his family from the destruction of the flood, it was his faith that acted upon God's revelation that saved his family from destruction. The work was the outcome of a faith that simply manifested an already existing way of living. The "ark" was simply *typical* of Christ. Noah had already trusted in the provision of which the "ark" typified long before he ever began building it, otherwise he would never have built it. His faith, and the salvation from the flood that it procured, was already his possession embryonically before the "ark" ever came into existence. Noah's "saving of his house" is the salvation of their lives through sanctifying obedience. Noah and his family's souls were already saved. Because they were already people of faith, they acted in sanctifying obedience that separated them from the rest of the world and led them to safety in the ark. This is the same context that we find in I Peter 3:18-4:11.

"[3:18] For Christ also hath once suffered for sins, the just for the unjust, that he might bring us to God, being put to death in the flesh, but quickened by the Spirit: [19] By which also he went and preached unto the spirits in prison; [20] Which sometime were disobedient, when once the longsuffering of God waited in the days of Noah, while the ark was a preparing, wherein few, that is, eight souls <u>were saved by water</u>. [21] <u>The like figure whereunto *even* baptism doth also now save us</u> (not the putting away of the filth of the flesh, but the answer of a good conscience toward God,) {*avowal of consecration to God after inquiry, having*

---

[37] *Pulpit Commentary*. SwordSearcher Software 6.1

repented and turned to God and now making this public proclamation of that fact by means of baptism[38]} by the resurrection of Jesus Christ: [22] Who is gone into heaven, and is on the right hand of God; angels and authorities and powers being made subject unto him. [4:1] Forasmuch then as Christ hath suffered for us in the flesh, arm yourselves likewise with the same mind: for he that hath suffered in the flesh hath ceased from sin; [2] That he no longer should live the rest of *his* time in the flesh to the lusts of men, but to the will of God. [3] For the time past of *our* life may suffice us to have wrought the will of the Gentiles, when we walked in lasciviousness, lusts, excess of wine, revellings, banquetings, and abominable idolatries: [4] Wherein they think it strange that ye run not with *them* to the same excess of riot, speaking evil of *you*: [5] Who shall give account to him that is ready to judge the quick and the dead. [6] For for this cause was the gospel preached also to them that are dead, that they might be judged according to men in the flesh, but live according to God in the spirit. [7] But the end of all things is at hand: be ye therefore sober, and watch unto prayer. [8] And above all things have fervent charity among yourselves: for charity shall cover the multitude of sins. [9] Use hospitality one to another without grudging. [10] As every man hath received the gift, *even so* minister the same one to another, as good stewards of the manifold grace of God. [11] If any man speak, *let him speak* as the oracles of God; if any man minister, *let him do it* as of the ability which God giveth: that God in all things may be glorified through Jesus Christ, to whom be praise and dominion for ever and ever. Amen" (I Peter 3:18-4:11).

Therefore, as we read I Peter 3:18-4:11, we must understand that an *already saved* man and his *already saved family* entered into the ark by faith. We must then understand that in I Peter 3:20, the phrase "eight souls were saved by water" is not referring to the point of their salvation from Hell or from condemnation. In fact, the word translated "saved" in the KJV is not from the Greek word *sozo* (sode'-zo), used everywhere else to refer to the salvation of the soul. The word translated "saved" in I Peter 3:20 is from the Greek word *diasozo* (dee-as-odze'-o). The idea of this verb is *to rescue, to escape from harm*, or *to keep*

---

[38] Robertson, Archibald Thomas. *Word Pictures in the New Testament, Vol. VI.* Grand Rapids: Baker Book House, 1930, 120.

safe. This is the way it is translated in Acts 23:24, 27:43, 44, 28:1 and 4. The meaning is that their lives were rescued from drowning in the floodwaters.

If we read the context of I Peter chapter three, it becomes obvious that the context of the text is about sanctification (I Peter 3:15), not salvation from Hell. The context of sanctification begins in chapter one and continues to the end of the epistle.

"Elect according to the foreknowledge of God the Father, through sanctification of the Spirit, unto obedience and sprinkling of the blood of Jesus Christ: Grace unto you, and peace, be multiplied" (I Peter 1:2 - CONTEXT).

"[13] Wherefore gird up the loins of your mind, be sober, and hope to the end for the grace that is to be brought unto you at the revelation of Jesus Christ; [14] As obedient children, not fashioning yourselves according to the former lusts in your ignorance: [15] But as he which hath called you is holy, so be ye holy in all manner of conversation; [16] Because it is written, Be ye holy; for I am holy" (I Peter 1:13-16 - CONTEXT).

"[1] Wherefore laying aside all malice, and all guile, and hypocrisies, and envies, and all evil speakings, [2] As newborn babes, desire the sincere milk of the word, that ye may grow thereby: [3] If so be ye have tasted that the Lord *is* gracious. [4] To whom coming, *as unto* a living stone, disallowed indeed of men, but chosen of God, *and* precious, [5] Ye also, as lively stones, are built up a spiritual house, an holy priesthood, to offer up spiritual sacrifices, acceptable to God by Jesus Christ" (I Peter 2:1-5 - CONTEXT).

"[19] For this *is* thankworthy, if a man for conscience toward God endure grief, suffering wrongfully. [20] For what glory *is it*, if, when ye be buffeted for your faults, ye shall take it patiently? but if, when ye do well, and suffer *for it*, ye take it patiently, this *is* acceptable with God. [21] For even hereunto were ye called: because Christ also suffered for us, leaving us an example, that ye should follow his steps: [22] Who did no sin, neither was guile found in his mouth: [23] Who, when he was reviled, reviled not again; when he suffered, he threatened not; but committed *himself* to him that judgeth righteously: [24] Who his own self bare our sins in his own body on the tree, that we, being dead to sins,

should live unto righteousness: by whose stripes ye were healed"
(I Peter 2:19-24 - CONTEXT).

"¹⁴ But and if ye suffer for righteousness' sake, happy *are ye*: and
be not afraid of their terror, neither be troubled; ¹⁵ But sanctify
the Lord God in your hearts: and *be* ready always to *give* an
answer to every man that asketh you a reason of the hope that is
in you with meekness and fear: ¹⁶ Having a good conscience;
that, whereas they speak evil of you, as of evildoers, they may be
ashamed that falsely accuse your good conversation in Christ. ¹⁷
For *it is* better, if the will of God be so, that ye suffer for well
doing, than for evil doing" (I Peter 3:14-17 - CONTEXT).

This leads us to the statement in I Peter 3:21, "The like
figure whereunto *even* baptism doth also now save us (not the
putting away of the filth of the flesh, but the answer of a good
conscience toward God,) {*avowal of consecration to God after
inquiry, having repented and turned to God and now making this
public proclamation of that fact by means of baptism*³⁹} by the
resurrection of Jesus Christ." The phrase "like figure" refers to
water baptism as a *type* of the *real thing*. The *real thing* is Holy
Spirit baptism, which refers to the supernatural act of God in
removing the *saved-by-faith* sinner from the cursed family of
Adam and supernaturally *regenerating* and *rebirthing* that *saved-
by-faith* sinner into the *New Genesis* ("the regeneration,"
Matthew 19:28).

Just as the family of Noah was separated from the
condemned family of Adam and the cursed first creation, all
believers are separated from the curse by baptism with the Holy
Spirit into the *New Creation*. Water baptism is a physical
portrayal of a believer's understanding of his *New Creation* "in
Christ" and his understanding of his responsibilities of that *New
Existence*. Therefore, water baptism is "the like figure" of Noah
and his family being saved by water. The picture, or type, is the
believer being separated from the curse by regeneration "by grace
through faith" and the baptism with the Holy Spirit. Faith and
salvation precede the *baptism* both actually and typically.
Therefore, water baptism is a physical portrayal of both *now* and
then realities of the believer's *New Existence*. In other words,

---

³⁹ Ibid.

there is a *now reality* to the believer's spiritual baptism that connects that believer to a *future reality* Eschatologically - glorification and ultimately to citizenship in the New Heaven/Earth, the final state of the *New Genesis* "in Christ." The now aspect of a believer's spiritual baptism connects him to all the responsibilities of his *New Existence* as a *Believer-Priest*.

Obviously, the context of the statement in I Peter 3:18- 4:11 is practical sanctification. Practical sanctification is the salvation of a believer's new life from being wasted. Without practical sanctification a believer would not be enabled to bring God glory through his *New Existence* (not merely the salvation of his soul). The context relates to practical sanctification in the supernatural enabling through yielding to the indwelling Christ (Romans 6:11-13). This is why we have the metaphorical use of the phrase "sprinkling of the blood of Jesus Christ" in I Peter 1:2. This metaphor is connected to the Old Covenant *sprinkling* in the typical sacrifice for the sanctification of Old Covenant believers. The sacrifice of Jesus and the shedding of His Blood is the *actual* sacrifice by which New Covenant believers receive this sanctifying "cleansing." This is what is referred to in the *actual* sense of cleansing, rather than the *typical* sense, in the first chapter of I John. This *sanctification cleansing* is intended to restore "fellowship" with God resulting in the filling/overflowing of the Spirit and the supernatural enabling of the believer "for the work of the ministry."

"[1] That which was from the beginning, which we have heard, which we have seen with our eyes, which we have looked upon, and our hands have handled, of the Word of life; [2] (For the **life** was manifested, and we have seen *it*, and bear witness, and shew unto you that **eternal life**, which was with the Father, and was manifested unto us;) [3] That which we have seen and heard declare we unto you, **that ye also may have fellowship with us**: **and truly our fellowship** *is* **with the Father, and with his Son** **Jesus Christ**. [4] And these things write we unto you, that your joy may be full. [5] This then is the message which we have heard of him, and declare unto you, that God is light, and in him is no darkness at all. [6] **If we say that we have fellowship with him**, and walk in darkness, we lie, and do not the truth: [7] But if we walk in the light, as he is in the light, we have fellowship one with another, and the blood of Jesus Christ his Son cleanseth us from all sin. [8] If we say that we have no sin, we deceive ourselves, and the truth is not in us. [9] If we confess our sins, he is faithful and just to forgive us *our* sins, and to cleanse us from all unrighteousness. [10] If we say that we have not sinned, we make him a liar, and his word is not in us" (I John 1:1-10).

Almost all Reformed theologians see the "confession" of I John 1:9 referring to the salvation *confession of sin.* There is no salvation *confession of sin*, although Calvin appears to make some form of distinction.[40] Some Reformed theologians refer to Bible texts on the *sprinkling with blood* as justifications for infant sprinkling (calling it infant baptism). The shedding of the Blood of Christ provides for both the remission of the penalty of all a believer's sins in the propitiation of God's wrath AND for sanctifying forgiveness that restores the sinning believer to fellowship with God. Both the salvation of the believer's soul from Hell and salvation of the believer's life through sanctifying cleansing are exposed in Hebrews chapter nine.

Roman Catholics make a false distinction in seeing some sins as *venial* and others as *mortal*. For Catholics, *mortal sins* are sins unto *spiritual death* (causing the sinner to lose *spiritual life*), resulting in separation from God. *Mortal sins* must be repented of and confessed to a priest before they can be forgiven in order to restore the sinner through the Sacrament of Penance. Catholics believe *venial sins* are lesser sins that are not sins unto death and do not require confession to a priest (although there is considerable ambiguity in Catholic literature defining *venial sins)*. *Venial sins* weaken the sinner, but do not cause him to lose *spiritual life*. It is hard for a Bible believer to make these distinctions when we understand that Adam's sin was simply eating something God that forbade. That simple act of disobedience brought God's curse upon all of the first creation.

---

[40] Calvin, John. *John Calvin's verse Commentary* (Sword Searcher Software 6.1)

Note: Calvin's beginning comments alludes to salvation, "[H]e again promises to the faithful that God will be propitious to them." He then goes on to say, "Thus he initiates that a twofold fruit comes to us from confession, — that God being reconciled by the sacrifice of Christ, forgives us, — and that he renews and reforms us." It is unclear if he understands the differentiation between salvation and the intent of the text as it refers to practical sanctification for "fellowship" with God.

DISCUSSION QUESTIONS

1. List and define the three aspects of salvation.

2. Why is it important to understand which of the three aspects of salvation a particular Bible text is referring?

3. After considering the statement in I Peter 3:18 through 4:11, was Noah already saved from spiritual condemnation when he was saved from physical destruction by the floodwaters?

4. Read I Peter 1:2, 13-16, 2:1-5, 19-24, and 3:14-17. Discuss the context of these portions of Scripture as they reveal water baptism connecting to practical sanctification rather than salvation.

5. Explain the phrase from I Peter 3:21, "The like figure whereunto *even* baptism doth also now save us (not the putting away of the filth of the flesh, but the answer of a good conscience toward God,) by the resurrection of Jesus Christ."

6. Read I John 1:1-10. Discuss the context of the *confession* of sins in I John 1:9. Is this *confession* salvational? Or, is this *confessional* for the purpose of sanctification and cleansing in order to restore broken fellowship with God?

7. Discuss the false view of *mortal* and *venial* sins and why this view distorts both salvation and sanctification.

BAPTISM
Chapter Seven
Can Infant Sprinkling Be Justified?

The so-called *Reformers* of Roman Catholic theology used some extreme logical presuppositions in order to justify infant baptism and later the sprinkling of infants. As we read their arguments for infant baptism and infant sprinkling, we must remember that they manufacture their interpretations of various Bible texts from the presupposition that infants were baptized in the early church (a fact that is not found anywhere in Scripture or anywhere in early church history as admitted by all honest Bible scholars). Therefore, these so-called *Reformers* were looking for Bible texts that *allowed* them to argue for their *already established practices*. After all, if they could not somehow justify their practices, that would mean they would all have to become *Anabaptists* (re-baptizers). They had been persecuting and murdering the *Anabaptists* for centuries. For them to admit that infant baptism/sprinkling was unscriptural would also be an admission to their heinous crimes against the *Anabaptists* that they and their predecessors committed. They used three Bible texts where Jesus allowed children/infants to be brought to Him to justify infant baptism/sprinkling. Their arguments in their use of these texts are ludicrous and ridiculous because the exegesis of these texts does not give any credence to their arguments.

"[13] Then were there brought unto him little children, that he should put *his* hands on them, and pray: and the disciples rebuked them. [14] But Jesus said, Suffer little children, and forbid them not, to come unto me: for of such is the kingdom of heaven. [15] And he laid *his* hands on them, and departed thence" (Matthew 19:13-15).

"[13] And they brought young children to him, that he should touch them: and *his* disciples rebuked those that brought *them*. [14] But when Jesus saw *it*, he was much displeased, and said unto them, Suffer the little children to come unto me, and forbid them not: for of such is the kingdom of God. [15] Verily I say unto you, Whosoever shall not receive the kingdom of God as {*like*} a little child, he shall not enter therein. [16] And he took them up in his arms, put *his* hands upon them, and blessed them" (Mark 10:13-16).

"[15] And they brought unto him also infants {*babes in arms*}, that he would touch them: but when *his* disciples saw *it*, they rebuked them. [16] But Jesus called them *unto him*, and said, Suffer little children to come unto me, and forbid them not: for of such is the kingdom of God. [17] Verily I say unto you, Whosoever shall not receive the kingdom of God as {*like*} a little child shall in no wise enter therein" (Luke 18:15-17).

Most people wrongly assume that every Christian denomination gets their theology from the exegesis of Scripture (biblical interpretation). As has been said previously, there were two basic theological positions of *Sola Scriptura* developing out of the Reformation. One said, *whatever the Bible does not disallow, we allow*. The other said, *whatever the Bible confirms, we confirm*. Therefore, there are many in professing *Christianity* with a *theology* of baptism that is completely separate from any exegesis of Scripture. For those holding to a true *Sola Scriptura* position, it is a complete *anathema* to try to establish a theological conclusion apart from direct exegesis of various Bible texts. Yet, this is a common practice of the supporters of infant sprinkling. The following quote from a leading Methodist theologian from years ago gives us an example of his understanding that *theology* can be separated from any exegetical support from Scripture:

> "J.R. Nelson affirmed: 'That the New Testament says nothing explicitly about baptizing of little children is incontestable. . . . In current discussion therefore greater weight must be placed for the defen[s]e of the practice upon theological rather than scriptural grounds.' *The Realm of Redemption*, pp. 129f."[41]

Almost all true Bible scholars of all denominations agree that there is no biblical support for baptizing (immersing) or sprinkling infants. Neither is there any true, honest Bible scholar that can find any example of anyone other than believers being

---

[41] Beasley-Murry, G. R. *Baptism In The New Testament.* Grand Rapids: William B. Eerdmans Publishing Company, 1973, 309.

baptized in the Scriptures. This is also exemplified by Reformed scholars at the turn of the twentieth century.

"In a review of Continental {European} work on baptism, Reider Bjornard suggested that the present era in baptismal discussions should be seen as beginning with Heitmuller's work, Im Namen Jesus, published in 1903.[2] Significantly that book was written in the conviction that baptism in the primitive Church was of believers only.[3] The same position was adopted in a very different work by F.M. Rendtorff, issued two years later,[4] by Feine in 1907,[5] and by Windisch in 1908.[6],[42] Item in { } added.

"Leenhardt, for example, in his valuable treatment of the New Testament teaching on baptism, wrote, 'It is generally agreed by defenders of infant baptism that the New Testament does not offer us explicit teachings capable of settling the problem of infant baptism. . . . It is the evidence of the facts which lead to this established position; *only the fanatics will contest it.*' He goes on to ask 'Why will people constantly take up arguments which have already been shown a hundred times to be untenable?'[8] This is indeed a startling reversal of the cry, '*Schwarmerer* –Fanatics!' addressed to the Anabaptists by both Lutherans and Reformed."[43]

We have numerous statements from many *Reformers* (probably better referred to as the *Confusers*) which use the statements of Jesus to justify allowing children to come to Him for *blessings* in Matthew 19:13-15, Mark 10:13-16, and Luke 18:15-17. Perhaps the classic statement is that of Calvin:

"*Suffer children.* He declares that he wishes to receive *children*; and at length, *taking them in his arms,* he not only embraces, but *blesses* them by the *laying on of hand;* from which we **infer** that his grace is extended even to those who are of that age. And no wonder; for since the whole race of Adam is shut up under the sentence of death, all from the least even to the greatest must perish, except those who are rescued by the only Redeemer. To exclude from the grace of redemption those who are of that age would be too cruel; and therefore it is not without **reason** that we

---

[42] Ibid., page 307.
[43] Ibid., page 307.

employ this passage as a shield against the Anabaptists. They refuse baptism to *infants*, because infants are incapable of understanding that mystery which is denoted by it. We, on the other hand, maintain that, since baptism is the pledge and figure of the forgiveness of sins, and likewise of adoption by God, it ought not to be denied to *infants*, whom God adopts and washes with the blood of his Son. Their objection, that repentance and newness of life are also denoted by it, is easily answered. *Infants are renewed by the Spirit of God, according to the capacity of their age, till that power which was concealed within them grows by degrees, and becomes fully manifest at the proper time. Again, when they argue that there is no other way in which we are reconciled to God, and become heirs of adoption, than by faith, we admit this as to adults, but, with respect to* infants*, this passage demonstrates it to be false.* Certainly, the *laying on of hands* was not a trifling or empty sign, and the prayers of Christ were not idly wasted in air. But he could not present the infants solemnly to God without giving them purity. And for what did he pray for them, but that they might be received into the number of the children of God? Hence it follows, that they were renewed by the Spirit to the hope of salvation. In short, by embracing them, he testified that they were reckoned by Christ among his flock. *And if they were partakers of the spiritual gifts, which are represented by Baptism, it is unreasonable that they should be deprived of the outward sign. But it is presumption and sacrilege to drive far from the fold of Christ those whom he cherishes in his bosom, and to shut the door, and exclude as strangers those whom he does not wish to be forbidden to come to him For of such is the kingdom of heaven. Under this term he includes both little children and those who resemble them; for the Anabaptists foolishly exclude children, with whom the subject must have commenced; but at the same time, taking occasion from the present occurrence, he intended to exhort his disciples to lay aside malice and pride, and put on the nature of* children. Accordingly, it is added by Mark and Luke, that no man *can enter into the kingdom of heaven* unless **he be made** to resemble a child. But we must attend to Paul's admonition, not to be children in understanding, but in malice, (**1Co** 14:20.)"[44] (Bolding and underlining added for emphasis.)

[44] Calvin, John. *John Calvin's Verse Commentary.* SwordSearcher Software 6.1.

This all appears to be a very *logical* argument for infant baptism/sprinkling. However, that is all it is. It is *logical*. **It is not biblical** (*Sola Scriptura*). A basic biblical truth is that all children of all nations (*not just the children of Jewish parents or of Christian parents*) are held innocent of sin by God until an unrevealed age/time when God begins to hold them accountable for their own fallen nature and their own sinfulness. In the Wilderness purging of Israel after their faith failure at Kadesh-Barnea, God held only those over the age of twenty accountable for the failure. We might hope this would be God's established *Age of Accountability*. It might be, but it is highly doubtful. The Zadokite Community (the Qumran Covenanters with which John the Baptist was identified and from which his rite of baptism is most probably derived) would not receive a disciple into their community until an individual reached the age of twenty years old.

"Whether or not infants were brought by their parents to the baptism of John [*the Baptist*] is beyond our ability to prove or disprove. It is impermissible, however, to insist that John must have followed the precedent of [*Jewish*] proselyte baptism in this respect, presuming that he knew it. We ought not to dismiss from the mind the fact that John's nearest neighbors, the Covenanters of Qumran, did not admit children to the lustrations. From the Two-column fragment we learn that children began to receive instruction in the teaching of the group when they became ten years of age, and they continued in it until they reached the age of twenty, at which time they became eligible for examination with a view to entering the community.[1] It is unnecessary to suggest that John followed in the steps of the Covenanters [*although this is the most probable*] in his administration of baptism as that he adhered to the procedure proselyte baptism when baptizing Jews, but it is worth reminding ourselves that there were other views in Judaism concerning the rightness of baptizing young children besides those which came to prevail in proselyte baptism. It is further necessary to recall the results of our comparison between John's baptism and proselyte baptism, for we found considerable differences between them: the strong eschatological element in John's baptism, referring both to judgment and hope, is absent from proselyte baptism, while the relation of proselyte baptism to the

Temple worship and to sacrifice in particular has no analogy to John's baptism. In both respects John is nearer to Qumran than to the proselytization of Jerusalem. But if the two rites, John's baptism and proselyte baptism, have so little in common, in their associations and significance, why should it be assumed as axiomatic that their conditions of administration were identical?"[45] (Items in [ ] added.)

Of course, the Dead Sea Scrolls (fragments of close to 1,000 scrolls with remnants of about 870 separate scrolls) and the Zadokite Documents were not available to the Reformers. They were discovered between the years 1946 and 1956 and were not really made available to anyone but the Roman Catholics until the early 1990's. The context of these documents probably provides a much stronger reason why John was call the "Baptist" other than merely his practicing of water baptism. It most probably refers to his association with the Zadokite Community, who were also known as *the Baptists*.

Granted, the idea that there was an inter-testament sect known as the *Baptist*s is a questionable conjecture. No one should propose that the Zadokites were a *Baptist denomination*. The term *denomination* cannot be used with the nomenclature *Baptist* because it denies a basic tenet of Baptist theology; i.e., the autonomy of a local assembly. True local, Baptist churches associated, affiliated, and fellowshipped together, but never formed *denominations*. Nonetheless, members of the Zadokite Community were known as the *Baptists*. Like the Anabaptists later, it was a name probably given to them by their contemporaries.

Studies of the three documents from the Dead Sea Scrolls, particularly the Damascus Document, the Habakkuk Pesher (Commentary), and the Community Rule, show us a community of inter-testament believers and their *understanding* of eschatological events surrounding the coming of Messiah. That does not assume these understandings were perfectly correct in that the Church Age was a mystery to the Jew.

---

[45] Beasley-Murry, G. R. *Baptism In The New Testament*. Grand Rapids: William B. Eerdmans Publishing Company, 1973,332.

The Zadokite Community would have come from the group of Jews that returned to Jerusalem under Nehemiah and Ezra. Ezra was a descendant of Zadok (Ezra 7:1-5), who was a descendant of Aaron, and therefore of the High Priestly line. This group of devout Jews returning from exile was referred to as the Sons of Righteousness (another name given to the Zadokite Community). Another title was the Hassidim (the Pious Ones). The word Essenes is most probably the Greek transliteration of the Hassidaeans. The etymology of Hassidim is from two words - Hesed (piety) and Zedek, which is a "dichotomy, descriptive of man's relationship to Deity, i.e., 'thou shalt love the Lord thy God.' Taken with the second, 'loving one's neighbor' or 'Righteousness towards one's fellowman', the two comprise the sum total of the 'commands of all Righteousness . . .'"[46]

All the various sects of Judaism at the time of Christ would have been descendants coming from the 42,360 Jews and their "servants and maids" (7,337; Ezra 2:64-65) that returned from exile. They all began as the Hassidaeans. When many of these Jews began to be Hellenized by the Greek culture, many others separated themselves from the Temple Order because they believed the priests ministering in the Temple were defiled. (The Damascus Document deals extensively with the "pollution of the Temple.").

During the time of the Hasmonean decadence and Roman conquest, the Zadokite Community increased in numbers. Therefore, there were many variations of sects within this sect (as there are among *Baptists* today).

The Dead Sea Scrolls were most probably deposited in the caves (where they were found) just before Herod's decimation of Qumran in about 37 BC (a severe earthquake occurred there in 31 BC). The site was vacant for over a generation. Many believe the group relocated its headquarters to Damascus during Herod's reign, later returning to Qumran. Many of these Zadokites (separatists) controlled the Sanhedrin until Herod the Great had all but two of them slaughtered. They were predominantly anti-Herodians.

---

[46] Eisenman, Robert. *The Dead Sea Scrolls and the First Christians.* Rockport, MA: Element Books Limited, 1996, 427.

Millar Burrows defines a number of the beliefs of the Zadokite Community:

1. They held the Scriptures in high esteem. The Law and the Prophets are quoted extensively in the Dead Sea Scrolls.
2. The leader of the *Community* was known as *The Teacher of Righteousness* who, it appears, was believed to have special interpretive abilities regarding the Scriptures. The result of this was that the interpretation of a text (like Habakkuk) was often interpreted in the light of recent historical events (and therefore distorted).
3. Entering the *Community* (formal membership) involved "taking an oath to return wholeheartedly to the Law of Moses." A considerable commitment was required of each covenanter to the study and interpretation of the Law. "Only within the community was true obedience to the law supposed to be possible."
4. "The sons of Aaron" (priests) governed the *Community*.
5. They believed in demonic forces of evil (the "angel of darkness") and the "Sons of Light" (i.e., righteousness). The defiled priesthood and their followers were referred to as the "men of Belial's lot." One of the Scrolls is "The War of the Sons of Light with the Sons of Darkness."
6. The *Damascus Document* divides the history of mankind "into five periods, in each of which God has set apart a saved remnant under the leadership of His chosen servants." This was a precursor to modern day Dispensationalism.
7. Election was viewed dualistically. True Israel was the "elect." Individuals became part of the "elect" group by becoming a covenanter in the *Community*.
8. The closing hymn of the *Manual of Discip*line reveals the *Community* members lived in "humble reliance" upon God.
9. The *Manual of Discipline* speaks of the coming of two Messiahs. These two Messiahs would rule Israel. One would be King and a descendant of king David. The other would be High Priest and a descendant of Zadok. The words "the Lord's anointed," from which the word Messiah originates, was applied to both the king of Israel and to the High Priest. Several references are made to "the Messiah of Aaron and

Israel" occur in the *Damascus Document*. The "Messiah of Aaron" would be the High Priest. The "Messiah of . . . Israel" would be the King. This application would have been in compliance with the Law's command against the High Priest and the King being one person.

10. Although they did believe in resurrection, they believed THEY would not be resurrected, but translated without death into the Kingdom of God. They referred to this as the "assumption." It is similar to what Dispensationalists believe regarding the Rapture.

11. They believed in eternal punishment in Hell for the "men of Belial" and "eternal joy in the life of eternity" for the "men of Light."

12. Justification by faith is somewhat difficult to see. In the Habakkuk Pesher it is said, "God will save those Jews who are *Torah-Doers* from *the House of Judgment* because of *their works and their faith* in the Righteous Teacher." This would be very close to what James teaches in James 1:22 and 2:14-26 and his teaching regarding Abraham's faith as exhibited by his work; i.e., his willingness to offer Isaac as a sacrifice to God.[47]

It is said by John M. Allegro, "Of all the recorded varieties of Judaism, that of the Essenes, as far as it is known, seemed the closest to the religion of the New Testament."[48] Claims that the Zadokite Community can be identified with Gnosticism and Zoroastrianism are really far-fetched.

Since there is undoubtedly an age of accountability that goes beyond infancy and toddler age, it is nonsense to try to justify some kind of *ritual* like infant baptism/sprinkling to *keep a child safe until he can believe for himself* (which is essentially the argument for the need of infant baptism/sprinkling in the first place). Therefore, all children of all kindred of people are SAFE until they reach an undetermined age when God begins to hold them accountable and when they must be "born again" to enter the kingdom of God.

---

[47] Burrows, Millar. *The Dead Sea Scrolls, Chapter XII*. New York: The Viking Press, 1957

[48] Allegro, John M. *The Dead Sea Scrolls and the Christian Myth*. Buffalo: Prometheus Books, 1992, 12.

THE INNOCENTS

The general premise of Reformed theology is to connect infant baptism or infant sprinkling with salvation to insure that children are *safe* until they believe. Their argument is that infant baptism is the sign of the New Covenant and it replaces circumcision as the sign of the Old Covenant. However, they fail to recognize that neither the Mosaic Covenant nor the New Covenant connect either circumcision or water baptism with salvation.

The *ordinances* of circumcision and water baptism are connected with *practical sanctification*, not salvation. Children do not need some invented ritual of infant baptism/sprinkling to make them *safe* from God's wrath should they die before believing. They are already *safe*. In the book of Jeremiah, God addresses the adults of Israel who had begun to practice Baalism, involving infant sacrifice to the pagan idol.

"[33] Why trimmest thou thy way to seek love? therefore hast thou also taught the wicked ones thy ways. [34] Also in thy skirts is found the blood of the souls of the poor innocents: I have not found it by secret search, but upon all these. [35] Yet thou sayest, Because I am innocent, surely his anger shall turn from me. Behold, I will plead with thee, because thou sayest, I have not sinned" (Jeremiah 2:33-35).

"[1] Thus saith the LORD, Go and get a potter's earthen bottle, and *take* of the ancients of the people, and of the ancients of the priests; [2] And go forth unto the valley of the son of Hinnom, which *is* by the entry of the east gate, and proclaim there the words that I shall tell thee, [3] And say, Hear ye the word of the LORD, O kings of Judah, and inhabitants of Jerusalem; Thus saith the LORD of hosts, the God of Israel; Behold, I will bring evil upon this place, the which whosoever heareth, his ears shall tingle. [4] Because they have forsaken me, and have estranged this place, and have burned incense in it unto other gods, whom neither they nor their fathers have known, nor the kings of Judah, and have filled this place with the blood of innocents; [5] They have built also the high places of Baal, to burn their sons with fire *for* burnt offerings unto Baal, which I commanded not, nor spake *it*, neither came *it* into my mind: [6] Therefore, behold, the days come, saith the LORD, that this place shall no more be called Tophet, nor The valley of the son of Hinnom, but The valley of slaughter" (Jeremiah 19:1-6).

In Jeremiah 2:34 and 19:4, God refers to these children as "innocents." This is translated from the Hebrew word *naw-kee'*, which literally means *exempt from guilt of sin*. Children do not need some invented ritual to make them *safe* from God's wrath in the event of premature death, because God Himself declares them *safe*.

We can see clearly from the Bible text about the death of king David's son from his adulterous relationship with Bathsheba that uncircumcised children, or infants never baptized, are safe. Two things we must note in reading II Samuel 12:15-23 are that the child died before he was eight days old (the age of circumcision) and that David says he will "go to him" in the afterlife.

"[15] And Nathan departed unto his house. And the LORD struck the child that Uriah's wife bare unto David, and it was very sick. [16] David therefore besought God for the child; and David fasted, and went in, and lay all night upon the earth. [17] And the elders of his house arose, *and went* to him, to raise him up from the earth: but he would not, neither did he eat bread with them. [18] And it came to pass on the seventh day, that the child died. And the servants of David feared to tell him that the child was dead: for they said, Behold, while the child was yet alive, we spake unto him, and he would not hearken unto our voice: how will he then vex himself, if we tell him that the child is dead? [19] But when David saw that his servants whispered, David perceived that the child was dead: therefore David said unto his servants, Is the child dead? And they said, He is dead. [20] Then David arose from the earth, and washed, and anointed *himself*, and changed his apparel, and came into the house of the LORD, and worshipped: then he came to his own house; and when he required, they set bread before him, and he did eat. [21] Then said his servants unto him, What thing *is* this that thou hast done? thou didst fast and weep for the child, *while it was* alive; but when the child was dead, thou didst rise and eat bread. [22] And he said, While the child was yet alive, I fasted and wept: for I said, Who can tell *whether* GOD will be gracious to me, that the child may live? [23] But now he is dead, wherefore should I fast? can I bring him back again? **I shall go to him**, but he shall not return to me" (II Samuel 12:15-23).

Notice that once the child was dead, David saw no need to mourn the child's death ("should I fast," v. 23) or to continue in lamentations over him. David understood that the child was *safe* with God in eternity. David understood that he would see his child again in eternity. Although there was a sense of *grief*, there was no *loss*. David knew where his child was. Although the child was never circumcised (or infant baptized), the child was *safe* in the presence and protection of the Creator.

Therefore, is infant baptism/sprinkling wrong or hurtful? This question takes us back to where we began.

"[1] At the same time came the disciples unto Jesus, saying, Who is the greatest in the kingdom of heaven? [2] And Jesus called a little child unto him, and set him in the midst of them, [3] And said, Verily I say unto you, Except ye be converted, and become as little children, ye shall not enter into the kingdom of heaven. [4] Whosoever therefore shall humble himself as this little child, the same is greatest in the kingdom of heaven. [5] And whoso shall receive one such little child in my name receiveth me. [6] But whoso shall offend {*the idea is to live in such a way or teach something that leads a child astray from 'the way,' John 14:6*} one of these little ones which believe in me, it were better for him that a millstone were hanged about his neck, and *that* he were drowned in the depth of the sea" (Matthew 18:1-6).

DISCUSSION QUESTIONS

1. Discuss why the Reformers sought so diligently to justify their practices of infant baptism when there is obviously no Scriptural support beyond *presuppositions*.

2. Define the two basic positions of *Sola Scriptura* produced from the Reformation.

3. Discuss the significance of the following quote as it reveals to us the differences between "theological" grounds for practices and "scriptural" grounds for practices in the minds of the Reformers.

> "J.R. Nelson affirmed: 'That the New Testament says nothing explicitly about baptizing of little children is incontestable. . . . In current discussion therefore greater weight must be placed for the defen[s]e of the practice upon theological rather than scriptural grounds.' *The Realm of Redemption*, pp. 129f."[49]

4. Comparing the statement of John Calvin given in this chapter to what Scripture says, what must be your conclusion regarding most of the so-called *theology* of John Calvin?

5. How do we know that John the Baptist and the Zadokite Community to which he was part, did NOT practice infant baptisms or infant sprinklings?

6. From Jeremiah 2:33-35 and 19:1-6, discuss why it is futile to baptize infants.

7. Read II Samuel 12:15-23. Did David either circumcise or infant baptize his son prior to his son's death? Did David believe he would see his son in Heaven?

---

[49] Beasley-Murry, G. R. *Baptism In The New Testament*. Grand Rapids: William B. Eerdmans Publishing Company, 1976, 309.

BAPTISM
Chapter Eight
The Bloody Waters of Baptismal Persecution

"[18] If the world hate you, ye know that it hated me before *it hated* you. [19] If ye were of the world, the world would love his own: but because ye are not of the world, but I have chosen you out of the world, therefore the world hateth you. [20] Remember the word that I said unto you, The servant is not greater than his lord. If they have persecuted me, they will also persecute you; if they have kept my saying, they will keep yours also. [21] But all these things will they do unto you for my name's sake, because they know not him that sent me. [22] If I had not come and spoken unto them, they had not had sin: but now they have no cloke for their sin. [23] He that hateth me hateth my Father also. [24] If I had not done among them the works which none other man did, they had not had sin: but now have they both seen and hated both me and my Father. [25] But *this cometh to pass*, that the word might be fulfilled that is written in their law, They hated me without a cause" (John 15:18-25).

Unknown to most Baptists today, true Christians paid a high price opposing the false doctrines of baptismal regeneration and infant baptism. Thousands upon thousands were slaughtered by Roman Catholicism during the Inquisition and thousands more were murdered later by the Reformers of Catholicism (perhaps they were not real Reformers after all). Thomas Armitage gives the following account of slaughter of a group that was known as the Albigenses in AD 1209 in his two volumes *The History of the Baptists*.

"They (the Roman Catholic army of 'half a million . . . barons, knights, counts, and soldiery') first attached Beziers, which was strongly fortified and garrisoned; but it was taken by storm and thirty thousand were slain. Seven thousand had taken refuge in the Church of St. Magdalene, and the monk Peter tells us with the most ferocious coldness they 'killed women and children, old men, young men, priests, all without distinction.' There were many Catholics in the town, and the 'Holy Legate' (leader of this Inquisition) was asked how these should be spared, when he commanded: 'Kill them all, God will know his own!' Lest a heretic should escaped they piled all in an indiscriminate heap, and the Chronicle of St. Denis gives the whole number as sixty thousand."[50] *Words in ( ) added*

The Albigenses were not Baptists, as we understand Baptists according to certain *doctrinal distinctives*, but they were an early group of Reformers that certainly rejected Rome's doctrine of baptismal regeneration. For this and other beliefs, the Inquisitors hunted them down and slaughtered them wherever they found them. A common way of executing the Anabaptists was to drown them in the same rivers in which they had been baptized. We find an account in *Foxes' Book of Martyrs* that exemplifies the terrorism of the Inquisition in Ireland.

"At the town of Issenskeath they hanged above a hundred Scottish Protestants, showing them no more mercy than they did to the English. M'Guire, going to the castle of that town, desired to speak with the governor, when being admitted, he immediately burnt the records of the county, which were kept there. He then demanded 1000 pounds of the governor, which, having received, he immediately compelled him to hear Mass. and to swear that he would continue to do so. And to complete his horrid barbarities, he ordered the wife and children of the governor to be hanged before his face; besides massacring at least one hundred of the inhabitants. Upwards of one thousand men, women, and children, were driven, in different companies, to Portadown bridge, which was broken in the middle, and there compelled to throw themselves into the water, and such as attempted to reach the shore were knocked on the head.

In the same part of the country, at least four thousand persons were drowned in different places. The inhuman papists, after first stripping them, drove them like beasts to the spot fixed on for their destruction; and if any, through fatigue, or natural infirmities, were slack in their pace, they pricked them with their swords and pikes; and to strike terror on the multitude, they murdered some by the way. Many of these poor wretches, when thrown into the water, endeavored to save themselves by swimming to the shore but their merciless persecutors prevented their endeavors taking effect, by

---

[50] Armitage, Thomas. *The History of the Baptists Traced by Their Vital Principles and Practices from the Time of Our Lord and Saviour Jesus Christ to the Year 1886 -Volume I*. Watertown, WI: Maranatha Baptist Press, 1980, 279.

shooting them in the water. . . . One hundred and fifteen men, women, and children, were conducted, by order of Sir Phelim O'Neal, to Portadown bridge, where they were all forced into the river, and drowned. One woman, named Campbell, finding no probability of escaping, suddenly clasped one of the chief of the papists in her arms, and held him so fast that they were both drowned together.

In Killyman they massacred forty-eight families, among whom twenty-two were burnt together in one house. The rest were either hanged, shot, or drowned. . . In Kilmore, the inhabitants, which consisted of about two hundred families, all fell victims to their rage. Some of them sat in the stocks until they confessed where their money was; after which they put them to death. The whole county was one common scene of butchery, and many thousands perished, in a short time, by sword, famine, fire, water, and others the most cruel deaths, that rage and malice could invent."[51] *Underling added.*

These people were slaughtered because they refused to recant their beliefs, one of which was the rejection of infant baptism and the heresy of baptismal regeneration. Would you be willing to give your life rather than deny the truth of the Gospel of Jesus Christ? Salvation is a gift of grace received through simple faith, and NOTHING ELSE. Christ viewed the denial of the faith response to the Gospel as denying Jesus Christ Himself.

By the early tenth century, Roman Catholicism dominated world politics and literally controlled nations and kings. True Christians were forced into hiding and obscurity, living in constant fear of being discovered and killed. Laws were passed in most European nations requiring the baptism/sprinkling of infants. The penalties for failure to comply were forfeiture of all property and often even a death sentence upon the parents. Even within this terroristic theater of existence there arose numerous sects that publicly taught against Rome's heresies. Such a man was Peter of Bruis. His followers came to be known as the *Petrobrusians.* These may have been true Baptists, not merely Anabaptists. Armitage gives us the distinction between the terms:

---

[51] *Fox's Book of Martyrs 19. Chapter XVII.* SwordSearcher Software 6.1.

"The term Cathari has also been applied to another thoroughly Baptist sect, which arose in the very dawn of the century [*the twelfth century*]: the PETROBRUSAINS. There leader was the great reformer, Peter of Bruis. In order to prevent confusion, it may be well here to define what is meant by the term 'Baptist,' when used to characterize one of these historical bodies. A Pedobaptist is one who baptizes babes. An Anti-pedobaptist is one who rejects the baptism of babes. But this does not of necessity make him a Baptist; for the Paulicians, Cathari, Albigenses, and in fact the modern Quakers, all cast infant baptism aside, but administered no baptism at all. Hence all these have rejected the baptism of babes as a matter of course, but we cannot, for that reason, number them with Baptists. An 'Anabaptist' is one who baptizes again for any reason. The Novatians and Donatists were 'Anabaptists' and reimmersed those who came to them from the Catholics. At the same time the Catholics were 'Anabaptists' when they reimmersed those who came to them from what they called the heretical bodies. They were therefore Pedobaptists and 'Anabaptists' at the same time. But a Baptist proper, in modern parlance, is one who rejects the baptism of babes under all circumstances, and who immerses none but those who personally confess Christ under any circumstances; and those who are thus properly immersed upon their faith in Christ, we have a right to claim in history as Baptists to the that extent, but no further."[52] *Words in [ ] added*

Armitage goes on to clarify why the *Petrobrusians* were considered true Baptists.

"In the Petrobrusians we find a sect of Baptists for which no apology is needed. Peter of Bruis seized the entire Biblical presentation of baptism, and forced [*used to imply dogmatism not coercion*] its teaching home upon the conscience and the life, by rejecting the immersion of babes and insisting on the immersion of all believers in Christ, without any admixture of Catharistic nonsense. . . He laughed at the stupidity which holds that a child is regenerated when baptized, that he can be a member of Christ's flock when he knows nothing of Christ as a

---

[52] Armitage, Thomas, *The History of the Baptists Traced by Their Vital Principles and Practices from the Time of Our Lord and Saviour Jesus Christ to the Year 1886 -Volume I.* Watertown, WI: Maranatha Baptist Press, 1980, 283.

Shepherd, and demanded that all who came to his churches should be immersed in water on their own act of faith. . . "[53]
Words in [ ] added.

We should question if Peter of Bruis were a genuine Baptist because in the next quote Armitage gives some of the beliefs of Peter of Bruis. It would appear that he did not disagree with Rome's view of baptismal regeneration. He simply disagreed with infants being baptized because their baptism could not be accompanied with their own faith. He had no objection to the Catholic's baptism of adults and did not require those adults to be baptized after they left Catholicism. Peter of Bruis said (as quoted by "the venerable monk, Maxima Biblioth"):

"The first article of the heretics denies that children below the age of reason can be saved by the baptism of Christ; and affirms that another's faith can do those no good who cannot yet exercise faith of their own, since, according to them, it is not another's but one's own faith which, together with baptism, saves, because the Lord said, 'Whosoever believeth and is baptized shall be saved.' He makes them say in another place, 'It is an idle and vain thing to plunge candidates in water at any age, when ye can, indeed, after a human manor, wash the flesh from impurities, but can by no means purify the soul from sins. But we await an age capable of faith, and after a man is prepared to acknowledge God as his and believe in him, we do not, as you slander us, *re*baptize, but baptize him; for no one is to be called baptized who is not washed with the baptism wherewith sins are washed away.'"[54]

At the least, there appears to be some ambiguity regarding the actual beliefs of Peter of Bruis in his understanding of the efficaciousness of water baptism. It appears he believed baptism efficacious when *accompanied by faith*.

Another group of Anabaptists suffered overwhelming persecutions at the hands of the Church of Rome. These were the Waldensians (believed to be named after an early leader named Peter Waldo, although there are those that claim this group traced

---

[53] Ibid., 285.
[54] Ibid., 287.

their heritage back to the Apostles). They were one of the first sects to translate the Bible from Latin into the *common language*. In response to the growing interest in reading these translations, the Church of Rome forbade anyone from reading the Bible or books explaining the Bible. This Roman Catholic ban on translations and reading Scripture would continue until Vatican II (in the early 1960's). Up until then, there was even a ban on reading any book not on the Roman Catholic list of approved books.

> "In order to stop this Christ-like proceedings of the Waldensians, the fourth Lateran Council, A.D. 1215, and the Council of Toulouse, 1229, forbade laymen to read the Bible either in the language of the people or in the Latin, and the Council of Tarragona, 1212, bound the prohibition on the clergy also."[55]

As these common *laypeople* began to read the Scriptures in their own language, more began to oppose Roman Catholicism's practice of infant baptism. The Church of Rome continued to persecute them and scatter them around Europe in an ongoing *Diaspora*. Although some individuals recanted under the overwhelming weight of persecution, many stayed true to the faith and died horrible deaths at the hands of their persecutors. Armitage gives one lengthy account of these persecutions in the city of Strasburg, France.

> "In 1212 a congregation of five hundred Waldensians was discovered at Strasburg. At first the bishop of that city sought to reason them out of their position against the Catholic faith; but such was their ready use of Scripture that disputations always inured to their advantage. Then he proclaimed that all of them who would not forsake their errors should be put to death by fire without delay. Many recanted, surrendered their books, and reported to him that they had three chief centers and three leaders – in Milan, in Bohemia, and on the ground in Strasburg. These leaders, they said. Were not clothed with the authority like the pope, but owed their influence to the personal confidence reposed in them by their brethren. One of their chief duties was to collect money for the poor. Eighty persons in all, amongst

---

[55] Ibid., 299.

whom were twenty-three women and twelve preachers, would not surrender their faith. John, the Strasburg leader, answered in the name of all. His appeal to Scripture could not be overthrown, and when his persecutors would apply the test of red-hot iron to see if he were sent of God, he replied; 'Thou shalt not tempt the Lord thy God.' 'Ah, he does not want to burn his fingers,' scornfully cried the monks. 'I have the word of God,' he answered, 'and for that I would not only burn my fingers but my whole body.' All who stood with him were put to death. Before their execution they were charged with all sorts of heresy, to which John replied from the Scriptures, moving the by-standers to tears. And when the final demand was made: 'Will you maintain your belief?' he replied, 'Yes, we will.' They were then led, amid the cries of kindred and friends, to the church-yard, where a broad and deep ditch had been dug. Into this they were driven, wood was piled around them and they perished in the flames. To this day men tremble when the 'Heretics Ditch' is pointed out in Strasburg."[56]

These extreme persecution events took place about three-hundred years before Martin Luther comes on the scene of the *Reformation* in AD 1517 with his writing of *The Ninety Five Theses*. Luther's *Reformation* was a completely different stream of *Reformation* than that which existed in the ongoing historical struggle by the numerous sects known as the Anabaptist against the theological heresies of Roman Catholicism. Although Luther is credited with rediscovering the doctrine of *justification by faith*, he really did not. He simply reduced the Roman Catholic sacraments from seven down to two – *infant baptismal regeneration* and *Consubstantiation* in the Holy Eucharist, rather than Rome's *Transubstantiation*. Therefore, this stream of the Reformation was almost always in apposition (reformation from within) of Roman Catholicism in its theological abuses and practices. These so-called *Reformers* continued Rome's views of Eschatology, Ecclesiology (especially *Theonomy*), Sacerdotalism, and Sacramentalism. These so-called *Reformers* also continued murdering and persecuting the Anabaptists. These ongoing persecutions were the outcome of their *Theonomic* worldview of the Kingdom. Most of them believed the Kingdom of God was

---

[56] Ibid., 300.

already in existence, or at least being brought into existence, in the *Theonomic Governance* of their various State Churches.

"Cardinal Hosius said truly that Luther did not intend to make all Christians as free as himself; thus, when they rejected his authority over their consciences, he treated them as the pope treated him; so Luther became a persecutor by slow degrees. He wrote to Spalatin, in 1522, concerning the Baptists: 'I would not have any who hold with us imprison them.'[8] In 1528 he also said: 'I am very sorry they treat the Anabaptists so cruelly, seeing it is only on account of belief, and not because of transgression of the laws. A man ought to be allowed to believe as he pleases. We must oppose them with Scriptures. With fire little can be accomplished.'[9] And still he sanctioned the degree of the Elector of Saxony, the same year, forbidding any but the regular ministers to preach or baptize, but under penalty of punishment.[10] Charles V. issued the terrible edict of Spire in 1529, commanding the whole empire to crusade against the Baptists. He ordered that: 'All Anabaptists, male or female, of mature age, shall be put to death, by fire, or sword, or otherwise, according to the person, without preceding trial. They who recant may be pardoned, provided they do not leave the country. All who neglect infant baptism will be treated as Anabaptists.' This was worse than any thing in mediaeval persecution, for at least the *form* of a trial had been observed; but the Protestant princes who assented to this edict left no way of escape, 'The design' being, as Keller says 'to hunt the Baptists with no more feeling than would be shown to wild beasts.'[11] The Peasant's War had only just closed when this ferocious edict was issued, yet it gives no hint that the Baptists were charged with sedition. The degree of 1529 was renewed in 1551, with this explanation: 'Although the obstinate Anabaptists are thrown into prison and treated with severity, nevertheless they persist in their damnable doctrine, from which they cannot be turned by any amount of instruction.'[12] If the remedy lay in 'severity' they ought to have been cured effectually, for everywhere they were treated much after the manner of serpents. A letter from a priest to his friend in Strasburg says: 'My gracious lord went hunting last Sunday, and in the forest near Epsig he caught twenty-five wild beasts. There were three hundred of them gathered together.'"[57]

---

[57] Ibid., 402.

These accounts show that the Baptists were dedicated and committed to the preservation of the Gospel of the gift of salvation "by grace through faith" apart from any rituals or human "works." They were fighting for the ongoing testimony of the central truth of the Gospel of Jesus Christ and they were willing to die rather than surrender. They understood that if they surrendered and allowed infant baptism and infant sprinkling to go on without correction that the very essence of the Gospel, and Christianity itself, was at stake. They were on the front lines of contending "for the faith once {*for all*} delivered to the saints" (Jude 1:3). They rightly saw themselves in the light of Scripture as the last bastion of hope in the fight against apostasy. Luther, Zwingli, Calvin, and Melancthon would continue this persecution.

> "Wigandus breathes the same spirit when he asks: 'Do you patiently protect such terrible enemies {*the Anabaptists*} of holy baptism? Where is your zeal for the house of God? Where such people as Jews and Anabaptists are tolerated there is neither grace nor blessing.'[14] Luther,[58] Zwingli[59] and Melancthon[60] uttered the severest things possible against them, without once stopping to show that their faith was contrary to the teachings of Jesus."[61] *Words in { } added.*

For centuries, these Baptists were hunted down, imprisoned, tortured, and slaughtered like animals. They had their properties confiscated and their children taken from them. They were burned at the stake, hung, drowned, tortured to death, and brutalized in ways that civilized people do not even mention and certainly could never imagine. Their persecutors burned their books. Their persecutors sought to eradicate every visage of Baptist beliefs from history. What was their horrible crime? They believed salvation was "by grace through faith" alone and that only those who were already saved and regenerate should be

[58] http://en.wikipedia.org/wiki/Martin_Luther (accessed 2/7/2-12)
[59] http://en.wikipedia.org/wiki/Huldrych_Zwingli (accessed 2/7/2-12)
[60] http://en.wikipedia.org/wiki/Philipp_Melanchthon (accessed 2/7/2-12)
[61] Ibid., 402.

baptized. Casper Schwenkfeld[62], who "was far from being a Baptist," writes:

"'The Anabaptists are all the dearer to me, that they care about divine truth somewhat more than many of the learned ones.' Then he candidly states what he understood the Baptists to believe, thus: 'The Old Covenant was a slavery, in so far as God, on account of man's perversity, constrained them to serve him. Hence, the sign of the covenant, circumcision, was put upon them before they desired it. They received the sign whether they were willing or not. But baptism, the sign of the New Covenant, is given only to those who, being brought by the power of God, through the knowledge of true love, desire it, and consent to follow true love. Unless loves forces them they should not be compelled.' Melancthon fell into the mistake of all history, in compelling infant baptism. It was all right with him that the Council of Nice ordered the rebaptism of Novatians, whether they desired it or not; but when the Baptists baptized a man on his own request, because of his love to Christ, he became at once the worst of all men and must welter in his own blood for his crime."[63]

All of these various sects of Anabaptists took the commands of the epistle of Jude as God's *voice* to them. They saw the sale of indulgences by the Roman Catholic clergy as the very fulfillment of which Jude warned. They saw infant baptism and baptismal regeneration as an enemy of the Gospel of salvation "by grace through faith" alone. They saw these aberrations and stood against them in true militancy. They were willing to die for the truth rather than compromise the Gospel.

"[3] Beloved, when I gave all diligence to write unto you of the common salvation, it was needful for me to write unto you, and exhort *you* that ye should earnestly contend for the faith which was once delivered unto the saints. [4] For there are certain men crept in unawares, who were before of old ordained to this

---

[62] http://en.wikipedia.org/wiki/Caspar_Schwenckfeld (accessed 2/7/2-12)
[63] Armitage, Thomas, *The History of the Baptists Traced by Their Vital Principles and Practices from the Time of Our Lord and Saviour Jesus Christ to the Year 1886 -Volume I.* Watertown, WI: Maranatha Baptist Press, 1980, 408.

condemnation, ungodly men, turning the grace of our God into lasciviousness, and denying the only Lord God, and our Lord Jesus Christ. [5] I will therefore put you in remembrance, though ye once knew this, how that the Lord, having saved the people out of the land of Egypt, afterward destroyed them that believed not. [6] And the angels which kept not their first estate, but left their own habitation, he hath reserved in everlasting chains under darkness unto the judgment of the great day. [7] Even as Sodom and Gomorrha, and the cities about them in like manner, giving themselves over to fornication, and going after strange flesh, are set forth for an example, suffering the vengeance of eternal fire" (Jude 1:3-7).

This is true biblical, militant fundamentalism as opposed to the *Fundamentalist Movement*. The *Fundamentalist Movement* did not list infant baptism and infant sprinkling as an anathema contrary to the fundamentals of the faith. Although the *Fundamentalist Movement* rejected baptismal regeneration, they did not equally, and adamantly, reject infant baptism. *Historic fundamentalism* has always rejected any acceptance of infant baptism or infant sprinkling. The rejection of infant baptism and infant sprinkling was fundamental to "the faith which was once delivered unto the saints." Therefore, the *Fundamentalist Movement* included such Pedobaptists as Presbyterians, Congregationalists, Wesleyan Methodists, and other various sects that practiced varying degrees of *infant baptism* and *infant sprinkling* for various reasons. Some of the sects included in the *Fundamentalist Movement* allowed for either *infant baptism* or *infant dedication* depending on the parents' desire. That is why true, historic Baptists would never align themselves with the *Fundamentalist Movement*. Unlike the fallen angels referred to in Jude 1:6, true Baptists have always sought to keep "their first estate" in their relationship of doctrinal purity with Christ and His infinite Word. Allowing infant baptism in any form, or for any purpose, was a complete *anathema* against their view of the purity of "the faith which was once delivered unto the saints." Therefore, the moment a professed Baptist aligns himself in any way with someone, or some group that accepts infant baptism for any reason, that individual ceases to be a true Baptist and a true *historic fundamentalist*. *Historic fundamentalists*, true contenders for the purity of doctrine, would rather die than make such alliances, and **historically they did**!

A willingness to die for something is the defining factor between having convictions and having preferences. Baptists do not practice baptism of believers only by immersion because we believe it is the preferred way. Baptists baptize believers only by immersion because this is what the Bible commands (orthodoxy) and this was the historical practice throughout the book of Acts and all the Epistles (orthopraxy).

> "[28] And the LORD heard the voice of your words, when ye spake unto me; and the LORD said unto me, I have heard the voice of the words of this people, which they have spoken unto thee: they have well said all that they have spoken. [29] O that there were such an heart in them, that they would fear me, and keep all my commandments always, that it might be well with them, and with their children for ever! [30] Go say to them, Get you into your tents again. [31] But as for thee, stand thou here by me, and I will speak unto thee all the commandments, and the statutes, and the judgments, which thou shalt teach them, that they may do *them* in the land which I give them to possess it. [32] Ye shall observe to do therefore as the LORD your God hath commanded you: ye shall not turn aside to the right hand or to the left. [33] Ye shall walk in all the ways which the LORD your God hath commanded you, that ye may live, and *that it may be* well with you, and *that* ye may prolong *your* days in the land which ye shall possess" (Deuteronomy 5:28-33).

Sadly, for many professing Baptists today, water baptism by immersion is something they have a *take it or leave it* attitude about. Many professing Baptists have never *dug into* the Scriptures to discover the deep spiritual and practical significance of total yieldedness to Christ that water baptism is intended portray. Water baptism portrays death to the "Old Man" (Romans 6:6), buried with Christ, and risen with Christ (Colossians 2:12) to "walk in the newness of life" (Romans 6:4). Then, the believer with that depth of convictions commits to renew that vision of existence, to which we testify in baptism by immersion, throughout each moment of every day. There must be a commitment to never "turn aside to the right hand or to the left" in the depth of their understanding of water baptism. **"O that**

there were such an heart in them, that they would fear me, and keep all my commandments always, that it might be well with them, and with their children for ever" (Deuteronomy 5:29)! God is talking about a heart that has such depth of character in convictions that it would not hesitate to die rather than move to the right or to the left of what He commands. Anything less than this is departure from the straight line of the "old paths." Many Baptist today are becoming like the Jews to which Jeremiah was called to rebuke.

> "[16] Thus saith the LORD, Stand ye in the ways, and see, and ask for the old paths, where *is* the good way, and walk therein, and ye shall find rest for your souls. But they said, We will not walk *therein*. [17] Also I set watchmen over you, *saying*, Hearken to the sound of the trumpet. But they said, We will not hearken" (Jeremiah 6:16-17).

DISCUSSION QUESTIONS

1. Why do you suppose so many thousands of Anabaptists were willing to die over the ordinance view of water baptism following salvation? Would you die rather than allow people to believe that water baptism was a sacrament that procured salvation?

2. Over what doctrine were the vast majority of religious persecutions and murders committed during the Roman Catholic Inquisition?

3. Discuss the meaning of the term *Pedobaptist* as compared to the term *Anabaptist*.

4. Why would the Roman Catholics ban the reading of the Waldensians' common languages translation of the Bible from the Latin Vulgate?

5. What was different between Luther's *Reformation* and what had been taking place in various sects of the Anabaptists that existed prior to Luther?

6. Discuss the difference between *apposition* Reformation and *opposition* Reformation.

7. Discuss why adamantly and militantly opposing infant baptism is a fundamental of the Christian faith.

BAPTISM

Chapter Nine

The Watered Down Doctrine of Water Baptism

There are a number of Bible texts to which we might refer as *Ecclesiology in a nutshell*. One such text is Acts 2:37-47. A second such text is Ephesians 4:1-16. Another is I Timothy chapter three. The ordinance that connects the believer to uniting with a local church and the beginning of his own practical Ecclesiology is the ordinance of water baptism.

"[37] Now when they heard *this*, they were pricked in their heart, and said unto Peter and to the rest of the apostles, Men *and* brethren, what shall we do?[38] Then Peter said unto them, Repent, and be baptized every one of you in the name of Jesus Christ for the remission of sins, and ye shall receive the gift of the Holy Ghost. [39] For the promise is unto you, and to your children, and to all that are afar off, *even* as many as the Lord our God shall call. [40] And with many other words did he testify and exhort, saying, Save yourselves from this untoward generation. [41] Then they that gladly received his word were baptized: and the same day there were added *unto them* {*the local congregation at Jerusalem*} about three thousand souls. [42] And they {*those believers who were saved and baptized uniting them to formal and covenantal membership with the local church of Jerusalem*} continued stedfastly in the apostles' doctrine and fellowship, and in breaking of bread, and in prayers. [43] And fear came upon every soul: and many wonders and signs were done by the apostles. [44] And all that believed were together, and had all things common; [45] And sold their possessions and goods, and parted them to all *men*, as every man had need. [46] And they, continuing daily with one accord in the temple {*probably second story meeting rooms in the Temple; see Acts chapter three*}, and breaking bread from house to house {*there were no formal meeting places yet*}, did eat their meat with gladness and singleness of heart, [47] Praising God, and having favour with all the people. And the Lord added to the church daily such as should be saved" (Acts 2:37-47).

The word "added" in Acts 2:41 is translated from the Greek word *prostithemi* (pros-tith'-ay-mee), which means *to be joined* or *united together*. **In this context, the union is**

covenantal. Many of these individuals were not from Jerusalem. When they returned to their homes in other cities and nations, they would become the *seeds* for local churches to begin in many other cities. Most of these new converts would become foundational people for the early missionary journeys of Paul and Barnabas. As Paul and Barnabas started new local churches on their missionary journeys, they would meet and use these new converts.

Perhaps the greatest failure in understanding water baptism is the failure to understand the spiritual dynamic of the way water baptism connects the "born again" believer to the doctrine of the Church (Ecclesiology). Water baptism is intended to reflect a believer's understanding of an already accomplished spiritual reality in the "born again" believer's eternal and supernatural connection to the Person of Jesus Christ. Water baptism is a covenantal testimony to accountability defining the way a person lives should live. The covenantal testimony of agreement is only for believers "born again" of the Spirit of God. That covenantal testimony of agreement is primarily between the believer and the Lord Jesus Christ. Every believer will give account of his faithfulness to that covenantal testimony of agreement to the Lord Jesus at the Judgment Seat of Christ.

Almost all Greek Lexicons give the two primary definitions of the Greek word *baptizo* (bap-tid'-zo) as to either *dip* or *immerse*. In the context of theological meaning, as water baptism portrays Spirit baptism in Romans 6:1-10 and as water baptism portrays the believer's understanding of his salvation through faith in the Gospel as detail in I Corinthians 15:3-4, there are three aspects necessary in the ritual portrayal. These three aspects establish why the word *dip* is really the best translation of *baptizo* (bap-tid'-zo), in that to *dip* means to both immerse in water and to then remove from the water. This was the word used to signify the dyeing of a garment. Once the garment was dipped and removed from the dye, its color was changed.

In the believer's portrayal of salvation and his baptism with the Spirit, the three aspects of salvation are all portrayed by *dipping* in water. These three aspects of salvation are the salvation of the soul from Hell, the salvation of the spirit from corruption through practical sanctification and continual cleansing, and the salvation of the body through resurrection/translation in glorification. The mode of water baptism therefore must portray all three of these aspects of salvation.

1. Death in that the "old man" (the believer's sin nature) was crucified with Christ (Romans 6:6 and Colossians 2:20)
2. Burial with Christ (Romans 6:4) signifying the "putting off" (Ephesians 4:22) of the "old man" (Colossians 3:8-9)
3. Resurrection with Christ (Colossians 3:1) and the "putting on" (Ephesians 4:24) of the New Nature "in Christ" to "walk in the newness of life" (Romans 6:4) in the union and unity with Christ in the baptism with (I Corinthians 12:13), and filling of (Ephesians 4:3 and 5:18), the Holy Spirit

Because there is such a shallowness in understanding the spiritual significance of what is portrayed in water baptism, we have created generation after generation of extremely shallow Christians. To make water baptism merely a testimony of salvation is a great abuse of the ordinance. As has been said repeatedly in these studies, water baptism is connected to sanctification, not salvation. Secondly, that sanctification is always connected to formal local church membership. Sanctification within the *ecclesia* is the biblical pattern of the practice of water baptism throughout both the Old Testament and the New Testament.

We find this transition from positional sanctification in the believer's *standing* "in Christ" in Romans 5:2 leading into the teaching on practical sanctification through the supernatural enabling of the indwelling Holy Spirit in Romans chapter six. These verses are critical for teaching an individual the spiritual significance of a decision to be water baptized.

"[1] Therefore being justified by faith, we have peace with God through our Lord Jesus Christ: [2] By whom also we have access by faith <u>into this grace wherein we stand</u>, and rejoice in hope of the glory of God. [3] And not only *so*, but we glory in tribulations also: knowing that tribulation worketh patience; [4] And patience, experience; and experience, hope: [5] And hope maketh not ashamed; <u>because the love of God is shed abroad in our hearts by</u>

the Holy Ghost which is given unto us {*the yielded believer becomes a potential distribution center of God's grace*}" (Romans 5:1-5).

The phrase in Romans 5:2 is critical to our understanding of Spirit baptism -"into this grace wherein we stand {*continue or abide-in the sense of a new level of supernatural existence*}." First, we must understand that the word "grace" means the *potential* for the supernatural enabling of a believer's life. Then we can understand how water baptism is intended to portray the believer's understanding of *positional sanctification.* This understanding leads the believer to his entrance into this new supernatural existence and the potential for the release of the *Christ-life* through practical sanctification and the filling of the Spirit. Because the emphasis of water baptism is wrongly put upon a mere testimony of salvation (*looking backward*), most new converts miss the significance of water baptism as its intent is to give them a new vision (*looking forward*). The new *forward vision* that is part of a proper understanding of water baptism is that of a believer's supernatural potential as he learns to die daily to self and completely yield to the indwelling Spirit of God.

"[1] What shall we say then? Shall we continue in sin, that grace may abound {*the gift of God's supernatural enabling is not about living permissively or selfishly*}? [2] God forbid. How shall we, that are dead to sin, live any longer therein? [3] Know ye not, that so many of us as were baptized into Jesus Christ were baptized into his death? [4] Therefore we are buried with him by baptism into death: that like as Christ was raised up from the dead by the glory of the Father, even so we also should walk in newness of life. [5] For if we have been planted together in the likeness of his death, we shall be also *in the likeness* of *his* resurrection: [6] Knowing this, that our old man is crucified with *him*, that the body of sin might be destroyed, that henceforth we should not serve sin" (Romans 6:1-6).

Obviously, water baptism is intended to portray an understanding of certain absolutes necessary to being supernaturally enabled to live each moment of our lives in practical sanctification before God. To allow someone to be water baptized without their understanding of these absolute necessities is perhaps the greatest abuse to the beginning of that new life "in Christ." Therefore, explanation of water baptism should involve the in-depth explanation of three levels of commitment necessary to be a disciple of Jesus Christ.

There must be a commitment to die daily to the "old man."

> "I protest by your rejoicing which I have in Christ Jesus our Lord, I die daily" (I Corinthians 15:31).

> "[19] For I through the law am dead to the law, that I might live unto God. [20] I am crucified with Christ: nevertheless I live; yet not I, but Christ liveth in me: and the life which I now live in the flesh I live by the faith of the Son of God, who loved me, and gave himself for me. [21] I do not frustrate the grace of God: for if righteousness *come* by the law, then Christ is dead in vain" (Galatians 2:19-21).

> "[22] But the fruit of the Spirit is love, joy, peace, longsuffering, gentleness, goodness, faith, [23] Meekness, temperance: against such there is no law {*no limitations*}. [24] And they that are Christ's have crucified the flesh with the affections and lusts. [25] If we live in the Spirit, let us also walk in the Spirit" (Galatians 5:22-25).

There must be a commitment to ongoing repentance, confession, and cleansing of sin so as to live as much as is possible in perpetual "fellowship" with Christ.

> "[5] This then is the message which we have heard of him, and declare unto you, that God is light, and in him is no darkness at all. [6] If we say that we have fellowship with him, and walk in darkness, we lie, and do not the truth: [7] But if we walk in the light, as he is in the light, we have fellowship one with another, and the blood of Jesus Christ his Son cleanseth us from all sin. [8] If we say that we have no sin, we deceive ourselves, and the truth is not in us. [9] If we confess our sins, he is faithful and just to forgive us *our* sins, and to cleanse us from all unrighteousness" (I John 1:5-9).

> "[8] For ye were sometimes darkness, but now *are ye* light in the Lord: walk as children of light: [9] (For the fruit of the Spirit *is* in

all goodness and righteousness and truth;) [10] Proving what is acceptable unto the Lord. [11] And have no fellowship with the unfruitful works of darkness, but rather reprove *them*" (Ephesians 5:8-11).

There must be total and absolute yieldedness to the indwelling Holy Spirit of God and the will of God revealed through the Word of God.

"[7] For he that is dead is freed from sin. [8] Now if we be dead with Christ, we believe that we shall also live with him: [9] Knowing that Christ being raised from the dead dieth no more; death hath no more dominion over him. [10] <u>For in that he died, he died unto sin once: but in that he liveth, he liveth unto God</u> {*this is the twofold model and spiritual view of the believer modeled in water baptism*}. [11] **Likewise** reckon ye also yourselves to be dead indeed unto sin, but alive unto God through Jesus Christ our Lord. [12] Let not sin therefore reign in your mortal body, that ye should obey it in the lusts thereof. [13] Neither yield ye your members *as* instruments of unrighteousness unto sin: but yield yourselves unto God, as those that are alive from the dead, and your members *as* instruments of righteousness unto God. [14] For sin {*the sin nature*} shall not have dominion over you: for ye are not under the law, but under grace. [15] What then? shall we sin, because we are not under the law, but under grace? God forbid. [16] Know ye not, that to whom ye yield yourselves servants to obey, his servants ye are to whom ye obey; whether of sin unto death, or of obedience unto righteousness? [17] But God be thanked, that ye were the servants of sin {*the sin nature*}, but ye have obeyed from the heart that form of doctrine which was delivered you. [18] Being then made free from sin, ye became the servants of righteousness [19] I speak after the manner of men because of the infirmity of your flesh: for as ye have yielded your members servants to uncleanness and to iniquity unto iniquity; even so now yield your members servants to righteousness unto holiness" (Romans 6:7-19).

Obviously, a decision to be baptized is intended to connect a saved believer to a commitment to discipleship. Therefore, a baptism decision is actually an enrollment into God's ordained organization for discipleship, which is the local church. Water baptism is intended to be the entrance into the discipleship process. Water baptism introduces the believer to his covenantal agreement that defines New Covenant living and ministry within the context of a local church community. Clearly, Jesus taught these various levels of commitment necessary to being one of His true disciples.

> "[25] And there went great multitudes with him: and he turned, and said unto them, [26] If any *man* come to me, and hate not his father, and mother, and wife, and children, and brethren, and sisters, yea, and his own life also, he cannot be my disciple. [27] And whosoever doth not bear his cross, and come after me, cannot be my disciple. . . [33] So likewise, whosoever he be of you that forsaketh not all that he hath, he cannot be my disciple." (Luke 14:25-27, 33).

Water baptism connects the believer to a covenantal relationship in formal membership with the local "body of Christ," which in turn connects the believer to the ongoing process of discipleship within that local assembly. A commitment to discipleship is a commitment to learn the Word of God and live the Word of God through "the work of the ministry." The "work of the ministry" is to proclaim the Gospel, baptize those that are saved into local churches, and teach those that are baptized to "observe" (live or do) the teachings of Jesus. The "work of the ministry" is never separated from the sending authority of the local church. A person must be connected covenantally to the "body" of a local assembly in order to have authority to minister in the name of Jesus Christ as the "head" of that local assembly. Anything else is completely foreign to biblical practice.

Water baptism in its relationship to local church membership, represents Spirit baptism in its relationship to the "church of the first born" in the "general assembly and in "the regeneration." Jesus, in His incarnation, became a *new* and *last* Adam in the union of His humanity and deity. In His humanity, He succeeded where the first Adam failed. There are two Bible texts that, when read in conjunction with one another, give us the depth necessary to understand this radical dispensational transition in "the regeneration" (the "new creation" or New Genesis "in Christ'). We will not comprehend the covenantal responsibilities of water baptism within a local church assembly until we understand water baptism's spiritual reality in Spirit baptism.

> "[12] Giving thanks unto the Father, which hath made us meet {*aorist*} to be partakers of the inheritance of the saints in light: [13] Who hath delivered {*aorist*} us from the power of darkness, and hath translated {*aorist*} *us* into the kingdom of his dear Son: [14] In whom we have {*present*} redemption through his blood, *even* the forgiveness {*remission of the penalty*} of sins: [15] Who is the image of the invisible God, the firstborn {*pro-tot-ok'-os, in preeminence, not in time: see John 8:58-'Before Abraham was, I am'*} of every creature {*created being*}: [16] For by him {*the eternal, self-existent Son of God*} were all things created, that are in heaven, and that are in earth, visible and invisible, whether *they be* thrones, or dominions, or principalities, or powers: all things were created by him, and for him {*again, eternal preeminence or Lordship is implied*}: [17] And he is before {*used in the sense of above, or superiority*} all things, and by him all things consist. [18] And he is the head of the body, the church {*referring here to the "general assembly" rather than the local assembly*}: who is the beginning, the firstborn from the dead; that in all *things* he might have the preeminence. [19] For it pleased *the Father* that in him should all fulness dwell; [20] And, having made peace through the blood of his cross, by him to reconcile all things unto himself; by him, *I say*, whether *they be* things in earth, or things in heaven" (Colossians 1:12-20).

A.W. Tozer said, "In many churches Christianity has been watered down until the solution is so weak that if it were poison it would not hurt anyone, and if it were medicine it would not cure anyone!" This is certainly true regarding the doctrine of the Church. I believe *watered down* Christianity begins with a *watered down* view of water baptism.

In Colossians 1:15-17, the emphasis is on the ETERNAL BEING of Jesus. In Colossians 1:18-19, the emphasis turns to the present resurrected glory of the Incarnate One. Jesus is Lord of the Church (the "first fruits" of the New Creation). The "church" is composed only of people who have put their faith in the FINISHED WORK of Christ for their salvation (both living and dead). They have already been "born again" into this "kingdom . . . of light." The word "church" in Colossians 1:18 refers to the future resurrected and glorified body of believers that will rule and reign with Christ during His one-thousand year reign on earth. Nonetheless, the "kingdom . . . of light" is still in their present reality of existence along with this material world. However, salvation is not the only qualification for formal membership in a local church. Water baptism is intended to precede formal membership in a local assembly and portray the covenantal responsibilities of New Covenant Christianity in a commitment to become a disciple of Jesus. If we miss this significance of the ordinance of water baptism, we miss its primary purpose.

Jesus is "the beginning" (Colossians 1:18) of this New Creation. The emphasis of this text is not on the "church," but on the regeneration to this NEW LIFE (existence) - the New CREATION. Jesus is the beginning of the New Creation as the now eternal God\man. The intent of the discipleship process within the organism of a local assembly is to teach the enrolled disciple to know the Word of God and how to live the Word of God through the supernatural enablement of the indwelling Spirit of God.

> "Therefore if any man *be* in Christ, *he is* a new creature: old things are passed away *{aorist tense}*; behold, all things are become *{perfect tense}* new" (II Corinthians 5:17).

Jesus is the "firstborn out from among the dead" into this New Creation. In the death, burial, and resurrection of Jesus, what man sees as an *end*, God sees as a *beginning* of a New Genesis.

> "[51] Behold, I shew you a mystery; We shall not all sleep, but we shall all be changed, [52] In a moment, in the twinkling of an eye, at the last trump: for the trumpet shall sound, and the dead shall be raised incorruptible, and we shall be changed. [53] For this corruptible must put on incorruption, and this mortal *must* put on immortality. [54] So when this corruptible shall have put on incorruption, and this mortal shall have put on immortality, then shall be brought to pass the saying that is written, Death is swallowed up in victory. [55] O death, where *is* thy sting? O grave,

where *is* thy victory? [56] The sting of death *is* sin; and the strength of sin *is* the law. [57] But thanks *be* to God, which giveth us the victory through our Lord Jesus Christ" (I Corinthians 15:51-57).

It would be of little value to be Lord of a dead and condemned creation. Jesus died so we could become part of His New Creation. "All things" (Colossians 1:17) refers to both the spiritual and material universe including the "church." Spirit baptism places the "born again" believer into that New Creation. Discipleship teaches him how to live supernaturally in this world although he is no longer "of the world" (John 17:14). The words "might have pre-eminence" (Colossians 1:18) means Jesus is *made* Sovereign LORD. As the Son of God, He has always been Sovereign LORD. Colossians 1:18 is referring to Jesus as the new Federal Head of humanity in His restoration of Adam's lost dominion to Satan. This restoration of dominion will not happen until Christ takes Kingdom Age rule of planet earth and Satan is bound for the thousand years of the Kingdom Age. However, there is a present aspect of this *dominion restoration* in this present worldly existence. This present aspect is defined in the way individual believers make personal choices in submission to the will of God. That is what the word "might" means.

In Colossians 1:18, Jesus is also referred to as "the firstborn of all creation." This does not refer to Jesus being the first created being. "Firstborn" is a Hebraism - a Hebrew phrase, idiom, or custom that can only be understood by understanding the idiom or custom. Being the "firstborn" was a *position of priority*. Therefore, the "firstborn" was usually the oldest in the family and resultantly held the patriarchal position of priority ("preeminence," Colossians 1:18).

"[27] Also I will make him *{the Messiah} my* firstborn, higher than the kings of the earth. [28] My mercy will I keep for him for evermore, and my covenant shall stand fast with him. [29] His seed also will I make *to endure* for ever, and his throne as the days of heaven" (Psalm 89:27-29).

Therefore, Christ Jesus possesses this position as the "last Adam" (I Corinthians 15:45) and as the new *Federal Head* of the New Creation based on the fact He is the "image of God," or in essence is God. The first Adam was created in the "image of God," but that image was defaced in his fall into the corruption of sin. Water baptism signifies an understanding of a disconnect from the cursed Adamic family and a new connection to the family of God (John 1:11-12).

Since no one of the creation is older than the Creator, He holds the first patriarchal position of priority (Colossians 1:16). He became part of His creation by being born as a baby. "Image" refers to Jesus being a physical revelation of the "invisible God." "Firstborn" refers to, and amplifies, the fact that even though Jesus had a physical birth, He is *eternally preexistent*. According to Colossians 1:17, the material creation was not only brought into existence by Jesus, but the material world was also completely dependent upon Him for its continuing existence ("by him all things consist').

Therefore, a believer's baptism with the Holy Spirit is a baptism into the "new creation" of the last Adam and the "church of the first born." This "church of the firstborn" exists embryonically in local churches during the Church Age. The whole of the "church of the firstborn" will have its first assembly at the rapture (I Thessalonians 4:16-17). At that time, all believers from all individual local churches existing during the Church Age will be united in "the general assembly." Because Christians have a superficial understanding of what has happened to them in their baptism with the Spirit into the "body of Christ," they also have a superficial understanding of what water baptism is intended to portray. Water baptism portrays the connection the believer has to his covenantal responsibilities within the "body of Christ" in his local church.

"[18] For ye are not come unto the mount that might be touched, and that burned with fire, nor unto blackness, and darkness, and tempest, [19] And the sound of a trumpet, and the voice of words; which *voice* they that heard intreated that the word should not be spoken to them any more: [20] (For they could not endure that which was commanded, And if so much as a beast touch the mountain, it shall be stoned, or thrust through with a dart: [21] And so terrible was the sight, *that* Moses said, I exceedingly fear and quake:) [22] But ye are come unto mount Sion, and unto the city of the living God, the heavenly Jerusalem, and to an innumerable company of angels, [23] To the <u>general assembly</u> and church of the firstborn, which are written in heaven, and to God the Judge of all, and to the spirits of just men made perfect, [24] And to Jesus the mediator of the new covenant, and to the blood of sprinkling {*sanctification not propitiation*}, that speaketh better things than *that of* Abel. [25] See that ye refuse not him that speaketh. For if they escaped not who refused him that spake on earth, much more *shall not* we *escape*, if we turn away from him that *speaketh* from heaven: [26] Whose voice then shook the earth: but now he hath promised, saying, Yet once more I shake not the earth only, but also heaven. [27] And this *word*, Yet once more, signifieth the removing of those things that are shaken, as of things that are made, that those things which cannot be shaken may remain. [28] Wherefore we receiving a kingdom which cannot be moved, let us have grace, whereby we may serve God acceptably with reverence and godly fear: [29] For our God *is* a consuming fire" (Hebrews 12:18-29).

Water baptism connects the believer's thinking to the spiritual dynamic of his Kingdom Age responsibilities within the Church Age (Hebrews 12:28). Water baptism also disconnects the believer's thinking from this world and connects him Eschatologically to the future destruction of the original Adamic creation (Hebrews 12:25-27).

Water baptism is a testimony that unites a "born again" believer with other "born again" believers as *accountability groups* established within various local churches. This unity in the formal membership of a local church exists within the process of discipleship (Ephesians 4:1-32). This unity grows through the ongoing process of discipleship on three fronts of spiritual growth:

1. Unity in **doctrine** that is acquired through detailed teaching of the Word of God and personal study of the Word of God
2. Unity in missional **purpose** to reach the world with the Gospel of Jesus Christ, baptize those saved in the "name of the Father, Son, and Holy Spirit," and teach "them to observe all things," which defines the third front of unity
3. Unity in **practice**, which defines the ministry of a local church comprised of individuals who understand the

112

responsibilities of holy living and the obligations of their individual positions as believer-priests before God

Ephesians 4:1-32 is *Ecclesiology 101*. It is the exposition of God's intent in the ordination of the local church defined in its doctrine, purpose, and practice. This threefold "unity of the Spirit" can never exist in any believer's life until that believer first unites himself with a local church.

> "[14] These things write I unto thee, hoping to come unto thee shortly: [15] But if I tarry long, <u>that thou mayest know how thou oughtest to behave thyself in the house of God, which is the church of the living God, the pillar and ground of the truth.</u> [16] And without controversy great is the mystery of godliness: God was manifest in the flesh, justified in the Spirit, seen of angels, preached unto the Gentiles, believed on in the world, received up into glory" (I Timothy 3:14-16).

God has ordained the ministry of the local church as the central vehicle of discipleship. Although the *home* and *family unit* is a prominent institution within the plan of God, the Great Commission was given to the Church. Homes or family units are not the "pillar and ground of the truth." The local church is "pillar and ground of the truth." The two ordinances of water baptism and the Lord's Supper are local church ordinances administrated through the authority of local churches. There is no such thing scripturally as a *parachurch* organization today. Show me a ministry that emphasizes the home at the expense of deemphasizing the local church and I will show you an unscriptural ministry. Show me a mission organization that is not directly connected and submissive to the local church and I will show you a mission organization that is abortive to the ordained methodology of God. This is a fundamental doctrine. Water baptism is God's ordained ordinance that introduces every "born again" believer to live within this dynamic of obedience within and through local churches.

DISCUSSION QUESTIONS

1. Discuss the relationship of water baptism to the doctrine of the Church (Ecclesiology).

2. Discuss why it is critical for a believer to understand that his uniting with a local church is covenantal.

3. Discuss why the word "dip" is actually a better translation of the Greek word *baptizo* than the word immerse.

4. Discuss the context of Romans chapter six, which is practical sanctification as this text relates to believer's baptism and his supernatural enabling by the Holy Spirit.

5. Discuss the details of the various aspects of commitment that are to be communicated by a believer in his water baptism.

6. How does water baptism connect a believer to his authority to minister in his relationship to his covenantal responsibilities to his local church?

7. Discuss the relationship of water baptism as it connects a believer to the local church as an *accountability group* to one another in the process of discipleship and to the Lord Jesus Christ.

BAPTISM

Chapter Ten

Water Baptism and the Covenantal Connection
to the Local Church

The epistle to the Hebrews was written to Jewish believers. It was written to establish the absolute superiority of the New Covenant under the High Priesthood of Jesus Christ within the context of local churches as the ministering priesthood of all believers. Although the whole of the epistle to the Hebrews establishes this superiority of the New Covenant over the Mosaic Covenant, Hebrews chapters ten through thirteen draws the believer out of the sacerdotal and sacramental shadows portrayed in the Mosaic Covenant and its old priesthood and sacrifices. Then the writer of Hebrews draws the believer to the realities of the New Covenant in its new priesthood within the spiritual dynamic of discipleship and their individual ministry through the local church. This is God's New Covenant order for the administration of all "born again" believers. They are to enroll in formal membership to a local assembly through which they can fulfill their vocational calling (Ephesians 4:1) "in Christ."

At the time of the writing of Hebrews (AD 68), the Jewish Temple in Jerusalem was still standing with a ministering priesthood and with sacrifices still being offered (this Temple was destroyed by Rome in AD 70). Professing Jewish Christians were being enticed back to the Temple and its sacrifices by the argument that Christ died only for original sin. They were being told that if they sinned after they were saved, they still needed to offer the same old Mosaic Covenant sacrifices to remove their defilement before God. Therefore, these Jewish believers were being enticed to "forsake" the local church assembly to return to the Temple and Mosaic Covenant practices.

"[19] Having therefore, brethren, boldness to enter into the holiest by the blood of Jesus, [20] By a new and living way, which he hath consecrated for us, through the veil, that is to say, his flesh; [21] And *having* an high priest over the house of God; [22] Let us draw near with a true heart in full assurance of faith, having our hearts sprinkled from an evil conscience, and our bodies washed with pure water. [23] Let us hold fast the profession of *our* faith without wavering; (for he *is* faithful that promised;) [24] And let us consider one another to provoke unto love and to good works: [25] Not forsaking the assembling of ourselves together, as the manner of some *is*; but exhorting *one another*: and so much the more, as ye see the day approaching. [26] For if we sin wilfully after that we have received the knowledge of the truth, there remaineth no more sacrifice for sins, [27] But a certain fearful looking for of judgment and fiery indignation, which shall devour the adversaries. [28] He that despised Moses' law died without mercy under two or three witnesses: [29] Of how much sorer punishment, suppose ye, shall he be thought worthy, who hath trodden under foot the Son of God, and hath counted the blood of the covenant, wherewith he was sanctified, an unholy thing, and hath done despite unto the Spirit of grace" (Hebrews 10:19-29)?

Hebrews chapters ten through thirteen give us considerable instruction regarding the New Covenant responsibilities. Water baptism connects the believer to these responsibilities in the context of formal local church membership and in God consecrating believers to "the work of the ministry" (Ephesians 4:12 and Romans 12:1-2). These responsibilities continue in the discipleship process ordained through the *organism* and *organization* of a local church. Water baptism is the ordinance (God's ordained methodology) for formal entrance into the discipleship process within the context of formal local church membership. The failure to teach that water baptism is the connecting link to culpability for discipleship through formal membership in a local assembly is the grossest of failures regarding this ordinance.

There are those who connect the statement "Let us draw near with a true heart in full assurance of faith, having our hearts sprinkled from an evil conscience, and our bodies washed with pure water" in Hebrews 10:22 as justification for baptism by sprinkling. This certainly is not the intent of the text. This statement in Hebrews 10:22 is merely an extension of what has been already said in Hebrews 9:8-14.

"[8] The Holy Ghost thus signifying, that the way into the holiest of all was not yet made manifest {*unlimited access by all believers*}, while as the first tabernacle was yet standing: [9] Which *was* a figure {*type or shadow*} for the time then present, in which were offered both gifts and sacrifices, that could not make him that did the service perfect, as pertaining to the conscience; [10] *Which stood* only in meats and drinks, and divers washings {*the confusion comes from the use of baptismos, here translated 'washings' referring to all the various water rituals for sanctification in the Old Covenant*}, and carnal {*typical, in that they touched only the flesh*} ordinances, imposed *on them* until the time of reformation {*used to refer to the setting of a broken bone, i.e. the intent is to the sacrifice of Christ fulfilling all Old Testament promises regarding the propitiation of God and the justification of sinners 'by grace through faith'*}. [11] But Christ being come an high priest of good things to come, by a greater and more perfect tabernacle {*the New Creation*}, not made with hands, that is to say, not of this {*earthly*} building; [12] Neither by the blood of goats and calves, but by his own blood he entered in once into the {*Heavenly*} holy place, having obtained eternal redemption *for us.* [13] For if the blood of bulls and of goats, and the ashes of an heifer sprinkling the unclean, sanctifieth to the purifying of the flesh: [14] How much more shall the {*sprinkling of the*} blood of Christ {*used in a metaphorical sense to refer to after salvation forgiveness for restoring a repentant, confessing sinner to 'fellowship' with God*}, who through the eternal Spirit offered himself without spot to God, purge your conscience from dead works {*the ongoing Old Covenant continual rituals, that by the very nature of their continuation revealed that the conscience could not be assured of the full propitiation of God*} to serve the living God" (Hebrews 9:8-14)?

The context of *sprinkling* in Hebrews 9:13 relates to an Old Covenant ritual involving the ashes from the burnt carcass of a "red heifer" mingled with pure water and sprinkled upon an unclean *believer* for the purpose of sanctifying "to the purifying of the flesh." This sprinkling was a physical ritual intended to portray typically, that which was necessary spiritually to restore a *believer,* who had defiled himself by contamination/contact with something, or someone that was unclean. Once the unclean person was restored to cleanness, he was restored to fellowship with God and his service and sacrifices were once again acceptable to God. This text is referring to the typology of purification rituals *for believers.* Every part of the slain "red heifer" was burnt to ashes outside "the camp." This is not the same as New Covenant water baptism. The Morrish Bible Dictionary gives us considerable clarification regarding the *Red Heifer Offering*:

> "This was a unique offering. The red heifer was killed outside the camp, and its blood was sprinkled by the priest seven times directly before the tabernacle. The whole of the heifer was then burnt, and the priest cast cedar wood, hyssop, and scarlet into the burning of the heifer. The ashes were gathered up and laid in a clean place outside the camp. When the ashes were used, a person that was clean mixed in a vessel some of the ashes with running water, then he dipped hyssop into the water, and sprinkled the person, tent, etc., that was unclean. **It was a water of separation — a purification for sin.**
>
> The ordinance of the red heifer was an exceptional form of sin offering. **It had not atonement in view, but the cleansing by water of those who, having their dwelling and place in the camp, where Jehovah's sanctuary was, had become defiled by the way**: cf. Nu 5:1-4. Upon the basis of sin being condemned in the cross, it corresponds to 1Jo 1:9. The washing of the feet of those that are clean, as taught by the Lord in John 13 has this character of cleansing with water. The Holy Spirit applies, by the word, the truth of the condemnation of sin in the cross of Christ to the heart and conscience, to purify the believer, **without applying the blood again**. Nu 19; Heb 9:13. But John 13 goes further. The Lord applies the truth of His departure out of this world to the Father to the walk of His disciples."[64] (Bolding added.)

The analogy of Hebrews 9:8-14 is that the *once-for-all* offering of the Blood of Christ to the Father in the literal Holy of Holies in Heaven eternally propitiates God's wrath for the believer's sins, eternally justifies the believer before God, AND provides perpetual cleansing of the saved sinner through the saved believer's *moment-by-moment* repentance, and confession of sin. Therefore, to apply Hebrews 9:8-14 to justify the sprinkling of infants as some form of *baptism* is a complete misrepresentation of the text. It is a complete misrepresentation in that these purification rituals were only for

---

[64] Morrish, George. *Morrish Bible Dictionary, Red Heifer.* SwordSearcher Software 6.1.

believers and were never used in the way *infant sprinklers* try to apply them. Secondly, such an application denies the context of Hebrews 9:14 in that the *once-for-all* offering of the Blood of Christ is perpetually efficacious to cleanse (purify) the sinning believer and restore him to practical sanctification and fellowship with God (I John 1:7-9).

In seeking to separate themselves by degree from the Roman Catholic view of infant sprinkling, the Reformers sought numerous variations seeking biblical support for infant baptisms (some by immersion and others by sprinkling) by arguing that infant baptism replaced infant circumcision. After Calvin's statements rejecting Roman Catholic infant baptisms on the basis that they were not by immersion, or because defiled Roman Catholic priests administrated the baptisms, we find numerous arguments seeking to justify sprinkling as an acceptable mode of these infant baptisms.

Two other texts are offered as *proof texts* by Reformed theologians to support baptism by sprinkling (which is a contradiction in terms) –Ezekiel 36:24-29 and the reference to the Ezekiel text in Hebrews 10:15-22. Again, the Reformers completely miss the typology in dispensational transitions. As we read Ezekiel 36:24-29, we must understand the Eschatological chronology (the *when*) to gain the context of *what* the prophecy is saying. The Eschatological timeframe is at the very beginning of the Kingdom Age and refers to the complete fulfillment of Joel 2:12-32, which was partially fulfilled on the Day of Pentecost (for the Church) recorded in Acts chapter two. Therefore, this is a *Day of Pentecost* for national Israel.

"[24] For I will take you {*the New Covenant nation of Israel made up of 'born again' Jews saved during the Tribulation time and now entering the Kingdom Age*} from among the heathen {*the Gentile nations*}, and gather you out of all countries, and will bring you into your own land {*the Promised Land of the Palestinian Covenant*}. [25] Then will I sprinkle clean water upon you {*no ashes of a red heifer are included because the once-for-all sacrifice of Christ is 'finished.' This 'clean water' refers to the 'renewing,' Titus 3:5 and Romans 12:2, of these believer's minds by the illumination of the 'water by the Word,' Ephesians 5:26, through the operations of the Holy Spirit*}, and ye shall be clean {*pure or purified*}: from all your filthiness, and from all your idols, will I cleanse you. [26] A new heart also will I give you, and a new spirit will I put within you: and I will take away the stony heart out of your flesh, and I will give you an heart of flesh. [27] And I will put my spirit within you, and cause you to walk in my statutes, and ye shall keep my judgments, and do *them*. [28] And ye shall dwell in the land that I gave to your fathers; and ye shall be my people, and I will be your God. [29] I will also save you from all your uncleannesses: and I will call for the corn, and will increase it, and lay no famine upon you. [30] And I will multiply the fruit of the tree, and the increase of the field, that ye shall receive no more reproach of famine among the heathen. [31] Then shall ye remember your own evil ways, and your doings that *were* not good, and shall lothe yourselves in your own sight for your iniquities and for your abominations {*the Kingdom Age will be a time of shame for national Israel*}. [32] Not for your sakes do I *this*, saith the Lord GOD, be it known unto you: be ashamed and confounded for your own ways, O house of Israel. [33] Thus saith the Lord GOD; In the day that I shall have cleansed you from all your iniquities I will also cause *you* to dwell in the cities, and the wastes shall be builded" (Ezekiel 36:24-33).

The Reformers' beliefs regarding the Church (Ecclesiology) caused them to see all of God's promises to national Israel transferred to the Church. They viewed the Church as a universal (worldwide) Theonomic entity that would one day govern the world (Amillennialism). Therefore, they viewed themselves already in the Kingdom Age and their reformations as advancing their *Theonomic Universal State Church* to its appointed place of ultimate authority and rule over the whole earth. From that false perspective, they viewed the prophecies of Ezekiel chapter thirty-six as already fulfilled and they viewed themselves as the reformers who were *sanctifying the Name of God* in the world. In this view, they saw themselves justified in killing people that opposed their divinely appointed authority because they were merely *purging the kingdom of reprobates.*[65]   Bad theology leads to the grosses of offenses against our fellowman and then justifies those offenses.

The trouble with using Hebrews 10:22 to justify sprinkling as a form of baptism is that to do so one must take it out of the context of the previous verses in Hebrews chapter nine. The statement of Hebrews 9:15-28 also clarifies Ezekiel's prophetic statement regarding *sprinkling* with pure water without customary mingling of *sacrificial ashes* for *sanctification* (this sprinkling was not for salvation). In Hebrews 9:24-28, Jesus is presented as the Perfect Offerer and His Blood as the Perfect Offering for sin. To understand this, we must look at Hebrews 9:15-28.

"[15] And for this cause he is the mediator of the new testament, that by means of death, for the redemption of the transgressions *that were* under the first testament, they which are called might receive the promise of eternal inheritance. [16] For where a testament *is*, there must also of necessity be the death of the testator. [17] For a testament *is* of force after men are dead: otherwise it is of no strength at all while the testator liveth. [18] Whereupon neither the first *testament {Mosaic Covenant}* was dedicated without blood. [19] For when Moses had spoken every precept to all the people according to the law, he took the blood of calves and of goats, with water, and scarlet wool, and hyssop, and sprinkled both the book, and all the people, [20] Saying, This *is* the blood of the testament *{Mosaic Covenant}* which God hath enjoined unto you. [21] Moreover he sprinkled with blood both the tabernacle, and all the vessels of the ministry. [22] And almost all things are by the law purged with blood; and without shedding of blood is no remission. [23] *It was* therefore necessary that the patterns of things in the heavens should be purified with these; but the heavenly things themselves with better sacrifices than these. [24] For Christ is not entered into the holy places made with hands, *which are* the figures of the true; but into heaven itself, now to appear in the presence of God for us: [25] **Nor yet that he should offer himself often**, as the high priest entereth into the holy place every year with blood of others; [26] For then must he often have suffered since the foundation of the world: **but now**

---

[65] Calvin, John, *The Institutes of the Christian Religion.* Book Third in PDF: Christian Classics Ethereal Library, 582.
http://www.ccel.org/ccel/calvin/institutes.html (accessed 2/7/2012)

once in the end of the world hath he appeared to put away sin **by the sacrifice of himself**. [27] And as it is appointed unto men once to die, but after this the judgment: [28] So Christ was **once offered** to bear the sins of many; and unto them that look for him shall he appear the second time without sin unto salvation" (Hebrews 9:15-28).

This then leads us to the introductory statements in Hebrews chapter ten regarding the perfect, *once-for-all* sacrifice of Jesus.

"[10] By the which will we are sanctified through the offering of the body of Jesus Christ once *for all*. [11] And every priest standeth daily ministering and offering oftentimes the same sacrifices, which can never take away sins: [12] But this man, after he had offered one sacrifice for sins for ever, sat down on the right hand of God; [13] From henceforth expecting till his enemies be made his footstool. [14] For by one offering he hath perfected for ever them that are sanctified. [15] *Whereof* the Holy Ghost also is a witness to us: for after that he had said before, [16] This *is* the covenant that I will make with them after those days, saith the Lord, I will put my laws into their hearts, and in their minds will I write them; [17] And their sins and iniquities will I remember no more. [18] Now where remission of these *is, there is* no more offering for sin" (Hebrews 10:10-18).

The fact that Jesus has offered His Blood as the final, *once-for-all,* perfect sacrifice explains why God says through Ezekiel, "[25] Then will I sprinkle clean water upon you, and ye shall be clean: from all your filthiness, and from all your idols, will I cleanse you. [26] A new heart also will I give you, and a new spirit will I put within you: and I will take away the stony heart out of your flesh, and I will give you an heart of flesh. [27] And I will put my spirit within you, and cause you to walk in my statutes, and ye shall keep my judgments, and do *them*" (Ezekiel 36:25-27). This text does not teach baptism by sprinkling. This text teaches that Kingdom Age *sanctification* (as is Church Age sanctification, I John 1:7-9) is available based upon a finished work of redemption in the complete propitiation of God by the one offering of Jesus Christ (I John 2:2).

"[19] Having therefore, brethren, boldness to enter into the holiest by the blood of Jesus, [20] By a new and living way, which he hath consecrated for us, through the veil, that is to say, his flesh; [21] And *having* an high priest over the house of God; [22] Let us draw near with a true heart in full assurance of faith, having our hearts sprinkled from an evil conscience, and our bodies washed with pure water" (Hebrews 10:14-22).

The "house of God" (Hebrews 10:21) is not a physical structure such as a church house or a church meeting place. The "house of God" in the New Covenant is a living organism of "living stones" united together in a particular locality (local church) with definitive structure (congregational government), administrated by God gifted men (pastors/bishops/elders), and sharing common doctrine, purpose, and practice. This is not a contractual union in formal membership. This formal membership is a covenantal union. The first aspect of this covenantal union is the acknowledgement of, and submission to, the new High Priest who is Jesus Christ. This *headship* or *Lordship* of Christ as the only High Priest over local churches is represented by numerous metaphors:

Metaphor: "a figure of speech containing an implied comparison in which a word or phrase ordinarily and primarily used of one thing is applied to another."

It is important that when we understand the use of these metaphors and that we make the application to the local assembly or "general assembly" based upon the context of Scripture. In almost all cases, the metaphors are used of the local church, not the "general assembly." Spirit baptism unites a believer to the "general assembly." Water baptism formally unites a believer to a local assembly.

A Body of Which Jesus Is the Head

"And he is the head of the body, the church: who is the beginning, the firstborn from the dead; that in all *things* he might have the preeminence" (Colossians 1:18).

123

"[19] And what *is* the exceeding greatness of his power to us-ward who believe, according to the working of his mighty power, [20] Which he wrought in Christ, when he raised him from the dead, and set *him* at his own right hand in the heavenly *places*, [21] Far above all principality, and power, and might, and dominion, and every name that is named, not only in this world, but also in that which is to come: [22] And hath put all *things* under his feet, and gave him *to be* the head over all *things* to the church, [23] Which is his body, the fulness of him that filleth all in all" (Ephesians 1:19-23).

Obviously, a "body" is formally united with its other parts. To consider one's self part of a local church without formally uniting to the "body" destroys the metaphor.

A Building of Which Jesus Is the Cornerstone

"[19] Now therefore ye are no more strangers and foreigners, but fellowcitizens with the saints, and of the household of God; [20] And are built upon the foundation of the apostles and prophets, Jesus Christ himself being the chief corner *stone*; [21] In whom all the building fitly framed together groweth unto an holy temple in the Lord: [22] In whom ye also are builded together for an habitation of God through the Spirit" (Ephesians 2:19-22).

A local assembly is built with converts to Jesus Christ. Therefore, the primary requirement for formal unity with a local assembly is the *living testimony* of having been "born again." It is upon the truth of the Gospel and His commandments that the local assembly/congregation is built. The building blocks of the local assembly are saved sinners who build their lives through discipleship within the local assembly on the truths for living given by the Lord. Obviously, a "building" is formally united with its other parts. To consider one's self part of a local church without formally uniting to the "building" destroys the metaphor.

A Bride of Whom Jesus Is the Bridegroom

"[21] Submitting yourselves one to another in the fear of God. [22] Wives, submit yourselves unto your own husbands, as unto the Lord. [23] For the husband is the head of the wife, even as Christ is the head of the church: and he is the saviour of the body. [24] Therefore as the church is subject unto Christ, so *let* the wives *be* to their own husbands in every thing. [25] Husbands, love your wives, even as Christ also loved the church, and gave himself for it; [26] That he might sanctify and cleanse it with the washing of water by the word, [27] That he might present it to himself a glorious church, not having spot, or wrinkle, or any such thing; but that it should be holy and without blemish. [28] So ought men to love their wives as their own bodies. He that loveth his wife loveth himself. [29] For no man ever yet hated his own flesh; but nourisheth and cherisheth it, even as the Lord the church: [30] For we are members of his body, of his flesh, and of his bones. [31] For this cause shall a man leave his father and mother, and shall be joined unto his wife, and they two shall be one flesh. [32] This is a great mystery: but I speak concerning Christ and the church. [33] Nevertheless let every one of you in particular so love his wife even as himself; and the wife *see* that she reverence *her* husband" (Ephesians 5:21-33).

This is one of the strongest metaphors for formal local church membership. Surely, every wife would agree. God has a word for a man who wants to join with his wife without first formally uniting with her through the marriage covenant. That word is adultery.

The theological significance of this metaphor is that it details the intimate relationship between Jesus Christ and local assemblies of believers. However, that intimacy does not exist apart from formally uniting through the ordinance of water baptism. Obviously, a "marriage" is formally uniting two partners together. To consider one's self part of a local church without formally uniting to the "marriage" destroys the metaphor.

Within the context of the marriage metaphor, we find the obligation of the "bride" to keep herself doctrinally and morally pure until the "bridegroom" returns to take her home. The corruption of a local church by false doctrine or moral impurity is equal to spiritual adultery.

"[1] Would to God ye could bear with me a little in *my* folly: and indeed bear with me. [2] For I am jealous over you with godly jealousy: for I have espoused you to one husband, that I may present *you as* a chaste virgin to Christ. [3] But I fear, lest by any means, as the serpent beguiled Eve through his subtilty, so your minds should be corrupted from the simplicity that is in Christ. [4] For if he that cometh preacheth another Jesus, whom we have not preached, or *if* ye receive another spirit, which ye have not received, or another gospel, which ye have not accepted, ye might well bear with *him*" (II Corinthians 11:1-4).

An Inheritance of Which Jesus Is the Heir

"[1] God, who at sundry times and in divers manners spake in time past unto the fathers by the prophets, [2] Hath in these last days spoken unto us by *his* Son, <u>whom he hath appointed heir of all things</u>, by whom also he made the worlds; [3] Who being the brightness of *his* glory, and the express image of his person, and upholding all things by the word of his power, when he had by himself purged our sins, sat down on the right hand of the Majesty on high; [4] Being made so much better than the angels, as he hath by inheritance obtained a more excellent name than they" (Hebrews 1:1-4).

The Church Age believer's inheritance is to rule and reign with Christ as a kingdom of priests during the Kingdom Age. This is stated in Revelation 2:25-29. Understand, as we read this text, that it is Jesus speaking. Therefore, the personal pronouns "he" and "him" are referring to individual faithful believers.

"[25] But that which ye have *already* hold fast till I come. [26] And <u>he that overcometh, and keepeth my works unto the end, to him will I give power over the nations</u>: [27] And he shall rule them with a rod of iron; as the vessels of a potter shall they be broken to shivers: even as I received of my Father. [28] And I will give him the morning star. [29] He that hath an ear, let him hear what the Spirit saith unto the churches" (Revelation 2:25-29).

Another important factor in these verses is that there are conditions to receiving this "rule." Every "born again" believer from the Church Age will inherit a position as a priest under the Lord Jesus Christ during the Kingdom Age. However, ONLY faithful believers from the Church Age will be consecrated by Jesus Christ to "rule" with Him during the Kingdom Age. Those who are saved, but unfaithful, during the Church Age will inherit the Kingdom, but not the "rule" (Matthew 25:14-30). Water baptism is intended to connect the believer to a life of faithfulness. Therefore, in a believer's formal membership in a local assembly he accepts accountability for the faithfulness through congregational government and pastoral administration. Uniting to a local assembly is the FIRST STEP in faithful obedience to our High Priest.

"[14] For as many as are led by the Spirit of God, they are the sons of God. [15] For ye have not received the spirit of bondage again to fear; but ye have received the Spirit of adoption, whereby we cry, Abba, Father. [16] The Spirit itself beareth witness with our spirit, that we are the children of God: [17] And <u>if children, then heirs; heirs of God, and joint-heirs with Christ; if so be that we suffer with *him*</u>, that we may be also glorified together. [18] For I reckon that the sufferings of this present time *are* not worthy *to be compared* with the glory which shall be revealed in us. [19] For the earnest expectation of the creature {*creation*} waiteth for the manifestation of the sons of God. [20] For the creature {*creation*} was made subject to vanity, not willingly, but by reason of him who hath subjected *the same* in hope, [21] Because the creature {*creation*} itself also shall be delivered from the bondage of corruption into the glorious liberty of the children of God. [22] For we know that the whole creation groaneth and travaileth in pain together until now. [23] And not only *they*, but ourselves also, which have the firstfruits of the Spirit, even we ourselves groan within ourselves, waiting for the adoption, *to wit*, the redemption of our body" (Romans 8:14-23).

Part of the Church Age believer's inheritance is to be glorified with Christ as a kingdom of priests. However, that position does not automatically translate into being allowed to minister during the Kingdom Age as priests.

A Flock of Which Jesus Is the Shepherd

"[1] Verily, verily, I say unto you, He that entereth not by the door into the sheepfold, but climbeth up some other way, the same is a thief and a robber. [2] But he that entereth in by the door is the shepherd of the sheep. [3] To him the porter openeth; and the sheep hear his voice: and he calleth his own sheep by name, and leadeth them out. [4] And when he putteth forth his own sheep, he goeth before them, and the sheep follow him: for they know his voice. [5] And a stranger will they not follow, but will flee from him: for they know not the voice of strangers. [6] This parable spake Jesus unto them: but they understood not what things they were which he spake unto them. [7] Then said Jesus unto them again, Verily, verily, I say unto you, I am the door of the sheep. [8] All that ever came before me are thieves and robbers: but the sheep did not hear them. [9] I am the door: by me if any man enter in, he shall be saved, and shall go in and out, and find pasture. [10] The thief cometh not, but for to steal, and to kill, and to destroy: I am come that they might have life, and that they might have *it* more abundantly. [11] I am the good shepherd: the good shepherd giveth his life for the sheep. [12] But he that is an hireling, and not the shepherd, whose own the sheep are not, seeth the wolf coming, and leaveth the sheep, and fleeth: and the wolf catcheth them, and scattereth the sheep. [13] The hireling fleeth, because he is an hireling, and careth not for the sheep. [14] I am the good shepherd, and know my *sheep*, and am known of mine. [15] As the Father knoweth me, even so know I the Father: and I lay down my life for the sheep. [16] And other sheep I have, which are not of this fold: them also I must bring, and they shall hear my voice; and there shall be one fold, *and* one shepherd" (John 10:1-16).

Those whom Jesus has redeemed are His possession. He knows each one personally and promises to care for each one by leading them to a local church where He has called and is directing a pastor to feed them, watch over them, and care for them.

"[1] The elders {*presbuteros*}which are among you I exhort, who am also an elder, and a witness of the sufferings of Christ, and also a partaker of the glory that shall be revealed: [2] Feed the flock of God which is among you, taking the oversight *thereof*, not by constraint, but willingly; not for filthy lucre, but of a ready mind; [3] Neither as being lords over *God's* heritage, but being ensamples to the flock. [4] And when the chief Shepherd shall appear, ye shall receive a crown of glory that fadeth not away" (I Peter 5:1-4).

The *undershepherd* that is responsible for "feeding" the Shepherd's sheep is the pastor of each local church.

DISCUSSION QUESTIONS

1. Discuss the historical context of the epistle to the Hebrews in the enticement by the Judaizers to the Hebrew believers to "forsake" their local churches to return to the Temple and the Mosaic Covenant practices.

2. Discuss the connection of water baptism to local church membership and the baptized believer's responsibilities to the discipleship process within the local church.

3. Explain Hebrews 9:8-14, especially the typology of sprinkling. Discuss why this does not refer to water baptism.

4. Explain the Red Heifer Offering.

5. Explain Hebrews 9:14 in detail regarding the eternal efficaciousness of the *once-for-all* offering of the Blood of Christ.

6. Discuss Reformed Theology's errant view of the Church (Ecclesiology) and then discuss how this errant view affects their understanding of Ezekiel 36:24-33.

7. List and discuss the four biblical metaphors of the Church. Discuss how understanding these metaphors helps you to understand the responsibilities of the priesthood of the believer in your connection to the local church through water baptism.

BAPTISM

Chapter Eleven

Water Baptism in Its Covenantal Connection to the Believer's Responsibilities Regarding the Pastor/Teacher

In I Timothy 3:15, Paul says, "But if I tarry long, that thou mayest know how thou oughtest to behave thyself in the house of God, which is the church of the living God, the pillar and ground of the truth." This statement follows some very detailed qualifications for the officers of a local church (and their wives). We cannot separate the instruction of this chapter of Scripture from the context of congregational government into which every believer enters upon his water baptism and by formally uniting to a local assembly of believers. Every local church is a "house{*hold*} of God." Every local church is an embryonic representation of how believer-priests will govern the Kingdom Age. Just like every *household*, a local church has a God-ordained chain of command within it. A pastor/teacher and the deacons function in the *household of God* like a husband and wife function together in a family in relationship to their children. If the family unit is dysfunctional because of a poor relationship between a husband, wife, and their children, we can never expect them to do any better as leaders of *the household of God*.

"[1] This *is* a true saying, If a man desire the office of a bishop, he desireth a good work. [2] A bishop then must be blameless, the husband of one wife, vigilant, sober, of good behaviour, given to hospitality, apt to teach; [3] Not given to wine, no striker, not greedy of filthy lucre; but patient, not a brawler, not covetous; [4] One that ruleth well his own house, having his children in subjection with all gravity; [5] (For if a man know not how to rule his own house, how shall he take care of the church of God?) [6] Not a novice, lest being lifted up with pride he fall into the condemnation of the devil. [7] Moreover he must have a good report of them which are without; lest he fall into reproach and the snare of the devil. [8] Likewise *must* the deacons *be* grave, not doubletongued, not given to much wine, not greedy of filthy lucre; [9] Holding the mystery of the faith in a pure conscience. [10] And let these also first be proved; then let them use the office of

130

a deacon, being *found* blameless. [11] Even so *must their* wives *be* grave, not slanderers, sober, faithful in all things. [12] Let the deacons be the husbands of one wife, ruling their children and their own houses well. [13] For they that have used the office of a deacon well purchase to themselves a good degree, and great boldness in the faith which is in Christ Jesus. [14] These things write I unto thee, hoping to come unto thee shortly: [15] But if I tarry long, that thou mayest know how thou oughtest to behave thyself in the house{*hold*} of God, which is the church of the living God, the pillar and ground of the truth. [16] And without controversy great is the mystery of godliness: God was manifest in the flesh, justified in the Spirit, seen of angels, preached unto the Gentiles, believed on in the world, received up into glory" (I Timothy 3:1-16).

Water baptism is a New Covenant ordinance that is a decision by a believer that connects him to a commitment to all the New Covenant responsibilities of the priesthood of all believers united together in individual local churches. Therefore, water baptism apart from formally uniting one's self to a local church, congregational government, concentrated discipleship, and pastoral administration is completely foreign to New Covenant praxis during the Church Age. Each of these local churches has God ordained leadership (Titus 1:5) and a chain-of-command defining the administration of a local church and its missional purposes. Water baptism as the connecting link to formal membership in a local assembly then also connects that believer to accountability to pastoral administration of his discipleship. The outgrowth of that discipleship should begin to manifest itself in the practice of "the faith" (James 1:22) and consistent involvement in the missional purpose of the local church (Matthew 28:18-20).

"[18] And Jesus came and spake unto them, saying, All power is given unto me in heaven and in earth. [19] Go ye therefore, and teach all nations, baptizing them in the name of the Father, and of the Son, and of the Holy Ghost: [20] Teaching them to observe all things whatsoever I have commanded you: and, lo, I am with you alway, *even* unto the end of the world. Amen" (Matthew 28:18-20).

A pastor's role within a local assembly, and the role of all spiritual leadership, is to insure that every baptized member of a local assembly is actually engaged in his own discipleship and the missional purpose of the local church as a spiritual organism. Without some form of accountability to the commitment that a person makes in his water baptism, that commitment has no relevant significance and no accountability for spiritual progress. This is perhaps the greatest of all the failures of present local church governance – people refuse to be held accountable. Pastors, in an attempt to retain people, enter into aberrations of *covert discipleship* and *guilt-trips* becoming little more than *motivational speakers.* Rebellious church members refuse to give their professed pastors the authority over their discipleship and refuse to willingly becoming accountable to them for their spiritual growth. The pastors try to coexist with these rebels in an environment where they live under the constant threat of God's children *running away from home.*

The role of the pastor in a local church is defined by four Greek words in the Bible. Each of these four Greek words refers to the same office, but to different functions, or job descriptions, of that office. The qualifications of I Timothy 3:1-7 must be met before a congregation, through congregational government, acknowledges God's call upon a pastor to minister in the office of a pastor. However, once a local congregation acknowledges God's call upon a pastor, they are to submit to his leadership and to his discipleship in their lives.

The Four Words Used to Describe One Position of Leadership

There are four separate words used in the Scriptures to describe the one office or position of the ministry of Jesus' (the Chief Shepherd's) *undershepherd.* The emphasis of each of these terms is upon what the *undershepherds* are called of God to do, not upon the position they hold. If they do not fulfill their obligations in *function* and in *role,* the terms become meaningless. Until the roles of each term are carefully understood by every member of a congregation of believers, there will be much confusion in that local church. Each term defines the function and reveals the intent of how God wants these individuals to be used and viewed within the local church.

Pastor

The word *pastor* is seldom found in the New Testament, yet it is the most common term used to describe the spiritual leader of a local assembly. It is a word that is derived from the word *Shepherd*. It comes from the Greek word *poimaino* (poy-mah'-ee-no) and it refers to the *supervisory aspects* of a guardian or protector (see John 10:11 and I Peter 2:25) as a *Shepherd* over *sheep*. It is also translated by the word "feed" in various Scriptures. This is a metaphorical use of the word as it relates to the teaching ministry of a pastor as he *feeds* the life changing truths of God's Word. This word is translated "shall rule" in Matthew 2:6, Revelation 2:27, 12:5, and 19:15. In many other Scriptures the word is used to describe *feeding* (John 21:16, Acts 20:28, I Corinthians 9:7, I Peter 5:2, Jude 1:12, and Revelation 7:17). When Peter says, "feed the flock" (I Peter 5:2), he is describing the role of *pastoral care*. The word *poimaino* (poy-mah'-ee-no) has more to do with describing what the *function* of the "elder" is (I Peter 5:1) than with a position.

> "¹ The elders which are among you I exhort, who am also an elder, and a witness of the sufferings of Christ, and also a partaker of the glory that shall be revealed: ² Feed the flock of God which is among you, taking the oversight *thereof*, not by constraint, but willingly; not for filthy lucre, but of a ready mind; ³ Neither as being lords over *God's* heritage, but being ensamples to the flock. ⁴ And when the chief Shepherd shall appear, ye shall receive a crown of glory that fadeth not away" (I Peter 5:1-4).

The pastor, as the "shepherd," obviously carries a very rich metaphorical meaning. We certainly see the metaphor used to describe the Lord Jesus in the very familiar Psalm 23. As Psalm 23 describes the *shepherding* ministry of the Lord Jesus and His sheep, the metaphor is also transferred to the role of the *undershepherd* as an ongoing extension of the ministry of Christ through His gifted men given to local churches in the pastor/teachers (Ephesians 4:11).

Teacher

This is the Greek word *didaskalos* (did-as'-kal-os). It is used in conjunction with pastoral ministry and usually in conjunction with the word *preaching*. Teaching was what Christ admonished Peter to do when He said to him "feed my sheep." It has been said that teaching *aims at the head*, while preaching is teaching *aimed at the heart*. When a person is water baptized, his commitment in water baptism unites him with the missional purpose of that local church. He also unites to the God-called pastor/teacher of that local church and becomes accountable to learn and live the teachings of God's Word as directed by the pastor/teacher. Just as Jesus commands the pastor/teacher to "feed" His "sheep," the "sheep" are expected to receive that teaching and begin to assimilate it into living.

"[15] So when they had dined, Jesus saith to Simon Peter, Simon, *son* of Jonas, lovest thou me more than these? He saith unto him, Yea, Lord; thou knowest that I love thee. He saith unto him, Feed my lambs. [16] He saith to him again the second time, Simon, *son* of Jonas, lovest thou me? He saith unto him, Yea, Lord; thou knowest that I love thee. He saith unto him, Feed my sheep. [17] He saith unto him the third time, Simon, *son* of Jonas, lovest thou me? Peter was grieved because he said unto him the third time, Lovest thou me? And he said unto him, Lord, thou knowest all things; thou knowest that I love thee. Jesus saith unto him, Feed my sheep. [18] Verily, verily, I say unto thee, When thou wast young, thou girdedst thyself, and walkedst whither thou wouldest: but when thou shalt be old, thou shalt stretch forth thy hands, and another shall gird thee, and carry *thee* whither thou wouldest not. [19] This spake he, signifying by what death he should glorify God. And when he had spoken this, he saith unto him, Follow me" (John 21:15-19).

Didaskalos (did-as'-kal-os) is used in the sense of *discipleship by teaching* people the Word of God in order for them to grow spiritually (see Matthew 28:20). The ministry of the pastor/teacher is to teach the Word of God. That means he is to teach, explain, expound, expose, and apply the Word of God so the "sheep" can readily assimilate it into their own lives. This ministry of the pastor/teacher prepares the baptized disciple to "do the work of the ministry" and begin to replicate that ministry in the lives of his family, neighbors, and friends. This creates a local church actively engaging their culture with the Gospel of Jesus Christ.

> "[19] Go ye therefore, and teach all nations, baptizing them in the name of the Father, and of the Son, and of the Holy Ghost: [20] Teaching them to observe all things whatsoever I have commanded you: and, lo, I am with you alway, *even* unto the end of the world. Amen" (Matthew 28:19-20).

The method that God ordained for this *teaching* ministry was *preaching* (see I Corinthians 1:21). Because of this, the *teacher* also came to be known as a *preacher* (*kerux,* kay'-roox; see Romans 1:15-16; 10:14-15; and I Timothy 2:7).

Bishop

This is the "overseer" ministry of the pastor (see I Peter 5:2). This is the Greek word *episkope* (ep-is-kop-ay'). It denotes the *function* of a pastor as an *overseer* and refers to the administration of the local church. It does not denote a separate position beyond or above the position/function of the pastor. In Paul's instruction to the elders at Ephesus, he refers to their function as *overseers*.

> "[17] And from Miletus he sent to Ephesus, and called the elders of the church. [18] And when they were come to him, he said unto them, . . . [25] And now, behold, I know that ye all, among whom I have gone preaching the kingdom of God, shall see my face no more. [26] Wherefore I take you to record this day, that I *am* pure from the blood of all *men*. [27] For I have not shunned to declare unto you all the counsel of God. [28] Take heed therefore unto yourselves, and to all the flock, <u>over the which the Holy Ghost hath made you overseers</u>, to feed the church of God, which he hath purchased with his own blood" (Acts 20:17-18, 25-28).

Therefore, the office of the pastor includes the function of *overseership*. Accordingly, the pastor/elder is also referred to as the bishop. These are not separate offices, but different *functions* of the same office.

> "[1] This *is* a true saying, If a man desire the office of a bishop, he desireth a good work. [2] A bishop then must be blameless, the husband of one wife, vigilant, sober, of good behaviour, given to hospitality, apt to teach; [3] Not given to wine, no striker, not greedy of filthy lucre; but patient, not a brawler, not covetous; [4] One that ruleth well his own house, having his children in subjection with all gravity; [5] (For if a man know not how to rule his own house, how shall he take care of the church of God?) [6] Not a novice, lest being lifted up with pride he fall into the condemnation of the devil. [7] Moreover he must have a good report of them which are without; lest he fall into reproach and the snare of the devil" (I Timothy 3:1-7, see also Philippians 1:1).

This *overseership* of the pastor is the meaning of the term "rule over you" in Hebrews 13:7 and 17. It is extremely important that the pastor be allowed freedom in this position because God will hold him accountable for any failures of obedience in the local church that he administrates (13:17).

In some churches, deacons become co-administrators with the pastor(s). This is foreign to both the Scriptures and New Testament practice. As the administrator or *overseer*, the pastor oversees every ministry of the local church. He does not do all the work. He *oversees* it all, co-ordinates it all, and makes sure it stays true to the Word of God and *on track* for Christ.

Elder

The word "elder" comes from the Greek word *presbuteros* (pres-boo'-ter-os). It refers to an individual with *mature spiritual experience* and the ability to apply the Word of God with wisdom. It is not a position separate from the position of the pastor, but describes a central qualification of a pastor (see I Timothy 3:1-7 above) defining his spiritual maturity and his well developed self-discipline. Therefore, in the use of the word as the title of a position, it cannot be separated from the central qualification of the pastor. The word *presbuteros* describes spiritual maturity involving both the *knowledge of* and the *personal application of* the Word of God (see I Peter 5:1, Acts 14:23, 20:17, I Timothy 5:1 and 17, and Titus 1:5-7).

BEGINNING AT THE BEGINNING

When it comes to a pastor's calling, congregations commonly make major mistake. Many local church congregations mistakenly believe that *they* call a pastor. That is not true. God calls a pastor to a local church ministry. A congregation's vote is not an *election* of a pastor. A congregation's vote is to *confirm* their belief that God has called a particular pastor to lead them. Congregational Polity is based upon the presumption that the majority of a congregation will make spiritual decisions as led by the Spirit of God and will *vote the mind of Christ*.

Once God's call upon a pastor is *confirmed* by the vote of a congregation, the leadership (*overseership*) of that local church is to be *turned over* to that pastor's direction. As he spends some time in a locality, God will reveal to him the direction and changes that need to be made to move that local congregation forward in its spiritual growth and service to the Lord. As long as the pastor is not doing anything unscriptural, to resist him is to resist the Lord. However, it is the congregation's responsibility to insure that he remains Scriptural in his practices. His administration of the local church is to be purely biblical.

> "Remember them which have the rule over you, who have spoken unto you the word of God: whose faith follow, considering the end of *their* conversation" (Hebrews 13:7).

The word "remember" in Hebrews 13:7 sets the tone for God's instruction defining a congregation's first responsibility to their pastor (*undershepherd*). It is from the Greek word *mnemoneuo* (mnay-mon-yoo'-o). "Remember" means to be *constantly aware of this person*. "Remember" means to *continually think of and feel for him*. Interestingly, it is in the imperative mood, which means it expresses a command to the hearer to perform a certain action by the order and authority of the one commanding. Therefore, the word "remember" relates an absolute command of God demanding full obedience. Anything less is sin. Following a pastor's leadership is an obligatory responsibility that should be given meticulous consideration before choosing not to do so.

"Them which have the rule" is translated from the Greek word *hegeomai* **(hayg-eh'-om-ahee). The meaning centers upon the word "rule."** It refers to *leadership* or *overseer authority*; in this case, this *authority* is a divinely appointed one. When calling a pastor to a local church, Jesus transposes His *headship* over that congregation to the pastor. This word is in the participle mood, which means it is used as a verbal noun. That means this word defines the pastor's position and authority as God's o*verseer* of a local congregation.

I Peter 5:1-4 further defines the role of a pastor as the ruling "elder" in a local church.

"[1] The elders which are among you I exhort, who am also an elder, and a witness of the sufferings of Christ, and also a partaker of the glory that shall be revealed: [2] Feed the flock of God which is among you, <u>taking the oversight</u> *thereof*, not by constraint, but willingly; not for filthy lucre, but of a ready mind; [3] <u>Neither as being lords over</u> *God's* heritage, but being ensamples to the flock. [4] And when the chief Shepherd shall appear, ye shall receive a crown of glory that fadeth not away" (I Peter 5:1-4).

In I Peter 5:1, the word "elders" is from the Greek word *presbuteros* **(pres-boo'-ter-os). It was a word used of those who, in separate cities, managed public affairs and administrated justice.** Among the early Christians, it was used to describe those who presided over local assemblies of believers. The New Testament uses the terms *bishop, elders,* and *presbyters* interchangeably. The term "elder" ascribes mature spiritual experience and wise understanding to an individual. In this context, *what* they are also is *who* they are.

In I Peter 5:2, the words "feed the flock" give us part of God's *job description* **for His pastors.** The pastor (*poimen*) is

God's appointed *guardian* or *protector* over God's local flock. In the Old Testament, the strength of a house was dependent upon the strength of its leader. Jesus is the "Chief Shepherd" (*archipoimen*; ar-khee-poy'-mane). Jesus is the only authority higher than the pastor.

In I Peter 5:2, once a pastor is called to be the *Shepherd* of a local church, he is *commanded* to "take the oversight" of that local congregation. "Oversight" is from the Greek word *episkopeo* (ep-ee-skop-eh'-o). This is the bishopric function of the pastor. The pastor *oversees*, or *administrates* every ministry of the church. The pastor does not do all the work. The ruling elder/pastor oversees it all and co-ordinates it all. The ruling elder/pastor makes sure it stays true to the Word and on track for Christ. This individual is culpable to the Lord Jesus for everything he teaches and every decision he makes regarding the administration and ministry of a local church. To take away his authority to make decisions in the local church for which he is culpable is the grossest of abuses against a pastor.

The Error of Presbyterian Government

A local congregation is not administrated by a church board, a board of elders, or by a board of deacons. This argument comes forth through Reformed Ecclesiology in varying degrees. There are numerous arguments for various kinds of elders within what is known as Presbyterian Government. There are *Ruling/Leading Elders*. There are *Teaching Elders*. There are *Lay Elders* who are assigned various stewardship roles. All of these various *Elders* serve together and administrate the local church together through a *Board of Elders*. This is not Congregational Government. This is Representative Government. It may function, but it is unscriptural because it denies the functionality of the priesthood of all believers. Almost all spiritual decisions under Presbyterian Government are made by a handful of men.

Under Congregational Government, a local church may approve a number of men to serve as their pastors. However, they should always choose one of those pastors to be the senior pastor. In this case, the senior pastor would be the bishop of the other pastors as well as the bishop of the local congregation. In other words, he would direct and administrate the ministry of the other pastors/elders as he administrates all other aspects of a local church's ministry. In the chain of command, all pastors would have authority over the deacons. The deacons have authority over their delegated areas of responsibility. Sunday school teachers and music leaders have authority over their delegated areas of responsibilities. The senior pastor has *ultimate* administrative authority over every ministry of a local church. The congregation is the only authority greater than the senior pastor. Even then, they must function within the parameters of biblical commands.

Presbyterian Government contradicts the biblical pattern of a local church under the direction, administration, and leadership of one *shepherd* or multiplicity of *shepherds* (elders). Although there may be other pastors serving in any local church, there is always the senior pastor who ultimately administrates that local church. The pastor is not the church's "hireling" who is supposed to do all of the spiritual work of the church. He is not called of God to do all the praying, or all the yard work, or all the painting, or all soul winning, or all the visitation. He is called to "perfect the saints for the work of the ministry." In other words, he is called of God to train the congregation he leads to do *all* those things. He should do that training through laboring in "the word and doctrine" (I Timothy 5:17) and by "example" (Philippians 3:17). This all must be done by men who struggle with the same temptations and weaknesses as every other person in a local church. These men are not some half God and half men *super-saints*. They are flesh and blood just like every person in the pew. They are prone to hurt, bleed, cry, and *break* just like everyone else. These men are God's gifts to you. Treat them well!

"[11] And he gave {*as gifts*} some, apostles; and some, prophets; and some, evangelists; and some, pastors and teachers; [12] For the perfecting of the saints, for the work of the ministry, for the edifying of the body of Christ" (Ephesians 5:4-11-12).

140

According to I Peter 5:2, the pastor's ministry should not be "by constraint." It is not something a man should be forced into, or compelled by another person to do. It is not a *vocational choice.* It is a calling of God. Therefore, it must be done willing and voluntarily. Every congregation needs to be regularly reminded that their pastor is there because God has *compelled* him to be there. Once he is fully persuaded in his mind that this is God's will for him, he cannot leave that position regardless of how poorly he is treated, how carelessly he is compensated, or how miserably his people follow his leadership.

A pastor does not serve a congregation "for filthy lucre's sake." He is not in the pastorate merely for material gain or for power and position. That often means that congregations do not take adequate financial care of their pastor. A congregation should never ask a pastor to make more sacrifices than they are willing to make.

Clearly, there is an established pattern in the New Testament books revealing that each local church was to have at least one pastor/teacher/elder/bishop who was to administrate and shepherd the members of that unique local "body." The formal membership of each local church had common parameters that defined their uniting as a "flock." The pastor/teacher had specific duties regarding his ministry to each member within the "flock." Each formal member of the "flock" has moral responsibilities to follow the leadership of the men God ordained to teach them, counsel them, and direct them in their own individual ministries through the local assembly. In other words, individual members could not just do whatever they wanted to do in any way they wanted to do it. They needed to be prepared through teaching and become accountable to their pastor in what they wanted to do both in the local assembly and in their external outreach ministries.

"[11] Wherefore comfort yourselves together, and edify one another, even as also ye do. [12] And we beseech you, brethren, to know {*meaning to look upon in order to perceive*} them which labour among you, and are over you {*above you in rank or in the chain of command*} in the Lord, and admonish you {*guide, caution, or gently reprove*}; [13] And to esteem them {*love them personally - respect and follow their authority*} very highly in love for their work's sake. *And* be at peace among yourselves" (I Thessalonians 5:11-13).

Hebrews 13:17 says, "Obey them that have the rule over you, and submit yourselves: for they watch for your souls, as they that must give account, that they may do it with joy, and not with grief: for that *is* unprofitable for you." Here we see that pastors will give account to God for what they teach the *sheep* under their care and how they lead those *sheep* and protect those sheep against doctrinal error and spiritual attacks. The pastors are commanded to not be "lords over *God's* heritage, but being ensamples to the flock" (I Peter 5:3). They will be accountable to God for this as well. It is unreasonable and unfair to ask a man to *shepherd* your life and soul without formally joining the *flock* God has called him to *shepherd*. How can he be accountable for you if you are not willing to become accountable to his leadership? A man of God certainly is a pastor if God has called him to that ministry. However, he is not YOUR pastor until you formally unite with the *flock* he is called to *shepherd*.

When you have another family and their children visit you home, do you parent their children? Do you want these visiting children to call you *dad*? Of course you would not want either of those things. You parent the children that are directly submitted to you and are formally united with your family. They are the only children you allow to call you *dad*. In the "household of God," the pastor can't be expected to *shepherd* every *sheep* that comes wandering aimlessly into the *flock*. A good *shepherd* realizes that is not one of his *sheep* and will try to either purchase that *sheep* or help it find a *flock* to which it can unite. The *sheep* has to make a formal choice to become accountable to the *shepherd*. A *sheep* unwilling to make that commitment really has no *shepherd*. Simply put, before a *sheep* can call a certain pastor his *shepherd*, he must officially choose the *flock* to which he wants to unite and submit to the *shepherd* and the congregational government of the *flock*. Until that point in time, he is a *sheep* that is wandering astray even though he may regularly graze with a certain *flock*.

"³⁵ And Jesus went about all the cities and villages, teaching in their synagogues, and preaching the gospel of the kingdom, and healing every sickness and every disease among the people. [36] But when he saw the multitudes, <u>he was moved with compassion on them, because they fainted, and were scattered abroad, as sheep having no shepherd</u>. [37] Then saith he unto his disciples, The harvest truly *is* plenteous, but the labourers *are* few; [38] Pray ye therefore the Lord of the harvest, that he will send forth labourers into his harvest" (Matthew 9:35-38).

Many men have left the ministry because the *sheep* will not follow the *shepherd*. It is almost as if following the leadership of God's ordained pastor is some kind of new teaching. It is not! It is ancient. Yes, there are those pastors who have abused their positions and *lorded* when they should have been *leading*. Congregational government should correct them or remove them because these men disqualify themselves. These *sheep abusers* are no justification for treating all other pastors with mistrust and they are certainly no excuse for failing formally to unite with another flock that has a godly pastor. That kind of practice is unjust.

Just as the pastor will give account to God for how he *shepherds* the *sheep*, the *sheep* will give account to God for their submission to the *shepherd's* teaching. Pastors knew this when they were sitting in the pew. A pastor knows when a *sheep* understands this when they are sitting in the pew listening to preaching. The person that understands this, and who fears the Lord the way he should, listens intently and on purpose. He knows if the pastor teaches something and he does not *take it home* with him, he is going to answer to God for his carelessness. If the pastor offers him good counsel that he rejects, he knows he is going to answer to God for his carelessness. The man who understands his accountability for his pastor's leadership is going to weigh those kinds of decision very carefully and give the pastor the benefit of any doubt.

DISCUSSION QUESTIONS

1. Water baptism connects every believer to a local church and responsibilities of formal membership in a local church. Discuss how every local church is an embryonic representation of how believer-priests will govern during the Kingdom Age.

2. Explain I Timothy 3:1-16 from the context of your answer to the previous question.

3. Discuss the extended responsibilities to which a believer connects himself by being water baptized. Explain these responsibilities in their connection to congregational government, concentrated discipleship, and pastoral administration of the two aspects of a local church.

4. Discuss the extended responsibilities of every water baptized believer in his relationship to the fulfilling of the Great Commission through the ministries of his local church.

5. List, define, and discuss the four words that describe the role of the pastor within the local church. Discuss how each of these four words relates to you particularly as a formal member of a local church.

6. Explain in detail the responsibilities of every water baptized member of a local church as detailed by Hebrews 13:7 and 17.

7. Discuss why the error of Presbyterian Government is completely contrary to the priesthood of all believers and how it corrupts the responsibilities of local church membership.

BAPTISM
Chapter Twelve
Water Baptism as It Relates to the Doctrine of Separation

The Bible is a combination of various books, each inspired by God, involving God's progressive revelation of Himself and His prophetic plan for the world. Every book was like adding another perfect member to an already perfect choir with each new revelation singing in perfect harmony with those revelations and truths that preceded them. No doctrines in the Word of God contradict one another. If the harmony of God's revelation is going to exist, every doctrine of God's Word must exist in its connection with others in perfect purity of voice without any contradictions. Every individual doctrine serves its unique purpose in the choir of progressive revelation. This is certainly true of the doctrine of water baptism in its relationship to the doctrine of separation and the purity of the local church. Church, as both an *organization* and an *organism*, does not work apart from a formal membership united by the communal decision in water baptism and in the practical application of Congregational Government.

There is much discussion these days about whether God intends the doctrine of separation to maintain the purity of the Gospel or to maintain the purity of the Church. Even for those that might agree that maintaining the purity of the Church is God's primary purpose in the doctrine of separation, many of those agreeing cannot agree on exactly what defines the term Church. There certainly seems to be a complete disregard in these discussions, about the purpose of separation, for the High Priesthood of Jesus Christ as His ministry presently relates to local churches. Certainly, the High Priestly ministry of Christ in His seven epistles to the seven local churches in Revelation chapters two and three give us precedent to conclude dogmatically that Christ is teaching that separation is critical to the purity of the local church.

The purity of any local church begins with the purity of the Gospel she understands and proclaims. The first area of the purity of any local church is the purity of a *regenerated membership.* If the Gospel is corrupted, or a biblical response to the Gospel is corrupted, unregenerate people may be added to the membership of a local church. Infant baptism and baptismal regeneration are corrupted responses to the Gospel of Jesus Christ. This corruption filled various denominational churches with unregenerate people and kept them in their state of unregeneration by their continuing misplaced faith in a *sacramental ritual.* Therefore, the first line of defense against a corrupted membership in any local church is the careful examination of the understanding of the Gospel, and the faith response to the Gospel, of those seeking membership. Ultimately, the weight of responsibility for a pure local church, and the final decision to include anyone in the membership of a local church, is made through Congregational Government. Pastoral administration accomplishes the maintenance of the purity of any local church through Congregational Government as each individual member is held accountable for his practice of the doctrine of separation.

Obviously, water baptism is the connecting link and beginning point to the practical application of a number of other doctrines as they apply to the purity of local church membership, the discipleship of all believers in the local church, practical sanctification, and personal evangelism by the members of a local church. Therefore, water baptism is undoubtedly the initial step in the practice of biblical separation. Another thing that ought to be obvious and essential is understanding the significance of water baptism beyond its being merely a testimonial ritual regarding a person's salvation.

Ekklesia (ek-klay-see'-ah), the Greek word that is translated "church" in our KJV English Bibles, is undoubtedly one of the most misunderstood and misapplied words in our English language. The word is made up of the primary preposition *ek,* which means *out from* in the sense of origin, "the point whence action or motion proceeds."[66] *Ek* is used in conjunction with the Greek word *kaleo* (kal-eh'-o), which means *to call forth.* Together, these two Greek words refer to the calling

---

[66] Strong, Augustus. *Strong's Greek Dictionary.* Iowa Falls, IA: Riverside Book and Bible House, 1890, SwordSearcher Software 6.1.

of a group of believers in Jesus Christ out from the world to gather in an assembly. We find this meaning of a *call to assembly* as the common usage in Scripture. Therefore, the very nature of the word *Ekklesia* implies separation from the world. To understand the term apart from the nature of the *out calling from the world* is to corrupt its primary meaning and its initial position of purity from worldliness and false doctrines. The initial context of any local assembly is to assemble in purity *from the world*. We see this in Acts 19:30-41.

> "[30] And when Paul would have entered in unto the people, the disciples suffered him not. [31] And certain of the chief of Asia, which were his friends, sent unto him, desiring *him* that he would not adventure himself into the theatre. [32] Some therefore cried one thing, and some another: for the assembly {*ekklesia*} was confused; and the more part knew not wherefore they were come together. [33] And they drew Alexander out of the multitude, the Jews putting him forward. And Alexander beckoned with the hand, and would have made his defence unto the people. [34] But when they knew that he was a Jew, all with one voice about the space of two hours cried out, Great *is* Diana of the Ephesians. [35] And when the townclerk had appeased the people, he said, *Ye* men of Ephesus, what man is there that knoweth not how that the city of the Ephesians is a worshipper of the great goddess Diana, and of the *image* which fell down from Jupiter? [36] Seeing then that these things cannot be spoken against, ye ought to be quiet, and to do nothing rashly. [37] For ye have brought hither these men, which are neither robbers of churches, nor yet blasphemers of your goddess. [38] Wherefore if Demetrius, and the craftsmen which are with him, have a matter against any man, the law is open, and there are deputies: let them implead one another. [39] But if ye enquire any thing concerning other matters, it shall be determined in a lawful assembly {*ekklesia*}. [40] For we are in danger to be called in question for this day's uproar, there being no cause whereby we may give an account of this concourse. [41] And when he had thus spoken, he dismissed the assembly {*ekklesia*}" (Acts 19:30-41).

Although the three uses of the Greek word *ekklesia* in Acts 19:32, 39, and 40 all refer to a *public, secular assembly* rather than a *local church assembly*, the important thing we see in the use of *ekklesia* in these three uses is that it is used of an *assembly.* Therefore, the primary significance of *ekklesia* in its definition of a local church is about an *assembly* or *congregation.* A local church then exists in two dynamics:

1. *Called out* from the world to *assemble* for the primary purpose of being taught the Word of God to prepare each believer for evangelism
2. *Sent out* into the world to evangelize and make disciples

Since the times of Augustine, the doctrine of the Church (Ecclesiology) has been corrupted. The Reformers did little, if anything at all, to correct Augustine's perverted Ecclesiology. Although Augustine saw the Church as both visible and invisible, he taught that all of God's promises to the nation of Israel were now given to the Church. He based his view of the Church primarily upon his corrupted allegorical interpretations of prophecy and his false views of the end times (Eschatology). Augustine's book *The City of God* exposes his Theonomic view of the Church known as *Amillennialism.* In this view, Augustine rejected a literal 1,000 year reign of Christ in a future Kingdom Age. Instead, he proposed that the prophecies about the Kingdom Age had already been fulfilled (*Preterism*) and that Christ was ruling the world through the *holy Catholic Church* with the Pope as the *Vicar of Christ.* He taught that the *Catholic Church* would one day usher in complete rule in a new utopian *one-world* government and a new utopian *one-world* social order (*Theonomic Amillennialism*). In this view of the Church, people were initiated into this *holy Catholic Church* through water baptism as the first step in their salvation and entrance into the *Kingdom.* Augustine of Hippo (AD 354-430) and Thomas of Aquino (AD 1225-1274) were the two main writers of systemic Theology for centuries. Both of these men were Roman Catholics.

Martin Luther (AD 1483-1546), the man accredited with being the *father of the Reformation,* did not come on the scene until about 300 years later. Other than *Luther's Catechism,* the *1646 Westminster Confession of Faith* is one of the first theological documents (doctrinal statements) we have coming from the Reformation. Although we see some variations from

Augustine's Ecclesiology, there are still a number of aberrations even in this Reformed Roman Catholic view of the Church. Luther reformed very little. The *1646 Westminster Confession of Faith* is Reformed Theology's view of the Church.

"**I.** The catholic or universal Church, which is invisible, consists of the whole number of the elect, that have been, are, or shall be gathered into one, under Christ the head thereof; and is the spouse, the body, the fullness of Him that filleth all in all.

II. The visible Church, which is also catholic or universal under the Gospel (not confined to one nation, as before under the law), consists of all those throughout the world that profess the true religion; and of their children: and is the kingdom of the Lord Jesus Christ, the house and family of God, out of which there is no ordinary possibility of salvation.

III. Unto this catholic and visible Church, Christ hath given the ministry, oracles, and ordinances of God, for the gathering and perfecting of the saints, in this life, to the end of the world; and doth by his own presence and Spirit, according to his promise, make them effectual thereunto.

IV. This catholic Church hath been sometimes more, sometimes less, visible. And particular Churches, which are members thereof, are more or less pure, according as the doctrine of the gospel is taught and embraced, ordinances administered, and public worship performed more or less purely in them.

V. The purest Churches under heaven are subject both to mixture and error: and some have so degenerated as to become apparently no Churches of Christ. Nevertheless, there shall be always a Church on earth, to worship God according to his will.

VI. There is no other head of the Church but the Lord Jesus Christ: nor can the Pope of Rome in any sense be head thereof; but is that Antichrist, that man of sin and son of perdition, that exalteth himself in the Church against Christ, and all that is called God."[67]

This *Big View* of Christianity as the *Church* is the view of the *Church* held by all Reformed churches, the vast majority of Evangelical churches, and now a large portion of fundamental

---

[67] *1646 Westminster Confession of Faith, CHAPTER XXV. Of the Church*
Online Publication:
http://www.reformed.org/documents/index.html?mainframe=http://www.reformed.org/documents/westminster_conf_of_faith.html (accessed 2/7/2012)

churches, even many Baptist churches. Nonetheless, it is an unbiblical view of Ecclesiology lacking an understanding of Dispensational transitions. It is also an impractical view of Ecclesiology because it lacks any connection to the obligations of Congregational Government in its responsibility to maintain the purity of its own regenerate membership. It lacks in teaching the responsibility of holding each member of a local assembly accountable for personal separation and moral turpitude. In most cases, this false Ecclesiology begins with a false understanding of water baptism as the entrance level into the formal membership of a local church. This false Ecclesiology continues in the failure to examine both a person's understanding of the Gospel and his obligations regarding personal separation from the world and unto God in practical sanctification in the "work of the ministry."

Obviously, the Westminster Confession sees the *Church* as something different from what we find defined by the Acts of the Apostles and epistles of the New Testament. Granted, there are portions of this statement with which we may heartedly agree, however the portions with which we disagree are a radical departure from the biblical norm. This becomes apparent in the thirty-five different times the word "churches" is used in the New Testament. This is especially true of the Revelation of Jesus Christ where He addresses the whole of that prophetic revelation to local "churches" throughout the Church Age in chapter twenty-two - "I Jesus have sent mine angel to testify unto you these things in the <u>churches</u>. I am the root and the offspring of David, *and* the bright and morning star" (Revelation 22:16). Christ does have a "general assembly" that He is building and will call to assemble at the beginning of the seven years of Tribulation (I Thessalonians 4:16-17). However, that Church is not yet complete and has not yet ever assembled. Until we understand that Dispensational transition, we will never be able to grasp Church Age Ecclesiology.

Although we have numerous *confessions of faith* (many links below[68]) from various sects of Anabaptists, most of these

---

[68] http://www.reformedreader.org/ccc/waldenses_confessions_of_faith.htm,
http://www.reformedreader.org/ccc/scf.htm, http://www.reformedreader.org/ccc/rr.htm
http://www.reformedreader.org/ccc/dcf.htm
http://www.reformedreader.org/ccc/hbd.htm (all accessed 2/7/2012)

lack any real definitiveness regarding Ecclesiology. In most part, there is not much in these documents that differentiate between the *Big View of Christianity* as the *Church*, except that they define Ecclesiology from the perspective of a regenerate and formally baptized membership. The 1527 Anabaptist document known as *Discipline of the Church*[69] does give some definitive statements regarding how a local church was to maintain its moral purity and obligations to one another within their own communion of faith. If we are going to understand the doctrine of the Ecclesiology, it is critical to differentiate between the Church *in the world* and the Church *glorified*. I have done this by using two different terms in these studies:

1. The local churches, meaning individual congregations of individual believers united covenantally through common salvation, common doctrine, common purpose, and common practice. These *local churches* are the *Church* of the Church Age.
2. The "general assembly" of "the church of the firstborn" (Hebrews 12:23), which is all believers of the Church Age first assembled in heaven at the resurrection/translation/glorification at the *catching away* of the Church (I Thessalonians 4:13-18). This is the *Church* of the Kingdom Age.

"[18] For ye are not come unto the mount that might be touched, and that burned with fire, nor unto blackness, and darkness, and tempest, [19] And the sound of a trumpet, and the voice of words; which *voice* they that heard intreated that the word should not be spoken to them any more: [20] (For they could not endure that which was commanded, And if so much as a beast touch the mountain, it shall be stoned, or thrust through with a dart: [21] And so terrible was the sight, *that* Moses said, I exceedingly fear and quake:) [22] But ye are come unto mount Sion, and unto the city of the living God, the heavenly Jerusalem, and to an innumerable company of angels, [23] To the general assembly and church of the firstborn, which are written in heaven, and to God the Judge of all, and to the spirits of just men made perfect, [24] And to Jesus the mediator of the new covenant, and to the blood of sprinkling, that speaketh better things than *that of* Abel. [25] See that ye refuse not him that speaketh. For if they escaped not who refused him

---

[69] http://www.reformedreader.org/dotc.htm (accessed 2/7/2012)

that spake on earth, much more *shall not* we *escape*, if we turn away from him that *speaketh* from heaven: [26] Whose voice then shook the earth: but now he hath promised, saying, Yet once more I shake not the earth only, but also heaven. [27] And this *word*, Yet once more, signifieth the removing of those things that are shaken, as of things that are made, that those things which cannot be shaken may remain. [28] Wherefore we receiving a kingdom which cannot be moved, let us have grace, whereby we may serve God acceptably with reverence and godly fear: [29] For our God *is* a consuming fire" (Hebrews 12:18-29).

The membership of the *Church in the world*, local congregations, is always banded together in *formal membership* defined as "born again" believers, baptized by immersion, living in harmony with the commands of the Word of God, committed to being disciples of Jesus Christ intent upon fulfilling the Great Commission, and having God called officers that meet biblical qualifications. The formal membership of the *Church in the world* biblically is always a local church and is governed by Congregational Government as each formal member of the *Body* discerns the *mind of Christ* (God's will) on any decision before them and they vote the *mind of Christ* (God's will). The formal membership constitutes a local church and is administrated by at least one pastor/teacher/bishop/elder (all in one person), who is *called* of God. God's calling of individual men, to administrate as the bishops of local churches, is to be spiritually discerned by the formal membership of a local church discerning the will of God and signifying that discernment by a congregational *vote of acknowledgment*. No individual member of any local church can rightfully abrogate his responsibilities regarding Congregational Government. Part of his membership obligations is to maintain a regenerate membership and the purity of the local church in its separation from worldliness.

The *Church glorified* (the "general assembly and church of the firstborn") is still being *built* (Matthew 16:18b-19a; "I will build my church; and the gates of hell shall not prevail against it. And I will give unto thee the keys of the kingdom of heaven"). The "general assembly" is often improperly referred to as the *Universal Church*. We cannot understand the differences between the *Church in the world* and

152

the *Church glorified* apart from understanding Dispensationalism and Dispensational transitions. For all practical purposes, the *Church glorified* does not yet exist in that it will not be assembled until after the resurrection/translation of Church Age believers when they will be glorified. The Church *glorified* is made up of all "born again" believers that are Holy Spirit baptized into the "body" of Christ (I Corinthians 12:13), indwelled, and sealed with the Holy Spirit of God from the Day of Pentecost to the beginning of the seven year Tribulation (I Thess. 4:16-17). The martyred Tribulation believers will be added to the *Church glorified* at the second coming of Christ (Revelation 20:4-6). The *Church glorified* will rule with Christ during the thousand year Kingdom Age on Earth as *kings and priests* with Christ.

The confusion of the *Church in the world* (the local church) and the *Church glorified* has led to much confusion in the interpretation of Scripture involving the issues of fellowship between local churches. This defines how local churches are to interrelate with one another through cooperative fellowship. The emphasis of Scripture regarding the local church is *internal purity*. The emphasis of Scripture regarding the *Church glorified* is *organic unity*. *Internal purity* is to be maintained through Congregational Government along with pastoral administration of the local church. *Internal purity* cannot be perfectly achieved in a sinful world. *Internal purity* involves attempting to maintain a purity of membership - only "born again" members united in spirit, doctrine, and purpose. Individuals will make false professions and become members of local churches. *Internal purity* involves maintaining purity in doctrine, purpose, and personal sanctification (holiness) of all individuals within a local church "body."

Organic unity of the *Church glorified* will be the natural spiritual dynamic upon glorification. Although various local churches may experience a degree of *organic unity* in fellowship with one another while *in the world*, *organic unity* will never be achieved in its purest sense during the Church Age, as it will be in the Kingdom Age. There also may be varying degrees of *organic unity* within a local church membership as each individual member of that local church seeks to live in habitual practical sanctification and the filling with the Spirit of God. *Organic unity* is not a mere organizational unity in structure and practice. *Organic unity* is deep "unity of the Spirit" of a local church membership as a living spiritual organism. Water baptism is the connecting link in the decisional process of separation from worldliness and separation unto God in "the work of the ministry."

Water baptism connects a believer to the maintenance of the internal purity of his local church by maintaining a *Believers Only* formal membership through Congregational Government - only "born again" believers were "added" to the Church.

> "[41] Then they that gladly received his word were baptized: and the same day there were added *unto them* about three thousand souls. [42] And they continued stedfastly in the apostles' doctrine and fellowship, and in breaking of bread, and in prayers. [43] And fear came upon every soul: and many wonders and signs were done by the apostles. [44] And all that believed were together, and had all things common; [45] And sold their possessions and goods, and parted them to all *men*, as every man had need. [46] And they, continuing daily with one accord in the temple, and breaking bread from house to house, did eat their meat with gladness and singleness of heart, [47] Praising God, and having favour with all the people. And the Lord added to the church daily such as should be saved" (Acts 2:41-47).

Water baptism connects a believer to the maintenance of the internal purity of his local church by maintaining a formal membership of only water baptized believers united and making purity decisions through Congregational Government about moral and doctrinal issues - only water baptized believers were "added to the church."

> "Go ye therefore, and teach all nations, baptizing them in the name of the Father, and of the Son, and of the Holy Ghost" (Matthew 28:19).

> "Then they that gladly received his word were baptized: and the same day there were added unto them about three thousand souls" (Acts 2:41).

154

"But when they believed Philip preaching the things concerning the kingdom of God, and the name of Jesus Christ, they were baptized, both men and women" (Acts 8:12).

Water baptism connects a believer to the maintenance of the internal purity of his local church by maintaining a formal membership through the Congregational Government of believers sharing a common faith (doctrine) that results in common practices –there is therefore accountability within the formal membership for learning the common faith and living the common practices (James 1:22).

"[4] There is one body, and one Spirit, even as ye are called in one hope of your calling; [5] One Lord, one faith, one baptism, [6] One God and Father of all, and in you all" (Ephesians 4:4-6).

"[9] Whosoever transgresseth, and abideth not in the doctrine of Christ, hath not God. He that abideth in the doctrine of Christ, he hath both the Father and the Son. [10] If there come any unto you, and bring not this doctrine, receive him not into your house, neither bid him God speed" (II John 9-10).

Water baptism connects a believer to the maintenance of the internal purity of his local church by maintaining a formal membership through Congregational Government in the careful selection of organized and Scriptural officers. It is the responsibility of individuals within local church membership to examine the Scriptural qualifications of those they are considering for spiritual leadership in a local church. Therefore, the formal membership of a local church must be taught these qualifications and be able to be discerning about the spiritual qualifications of individuals being considered.

"Paul and Timotheus, the servants of Jesus Christ, to all the saints in Christ Jesus which are at Philippi, with the bishops and deacons" (Philippians 1:1).

"[1] This *is* a true saying, If a man desire the office of a bishop, he desireth a good work. [2] A bishop then must be blameless, the husband of one wife, vigilant, sober, of good behaviour, given to hospitality, apt to teach; [3] Not given to wine, no striker, not greedy of filthy lucre; but patient, not a brawler, not covetous; [4] One that ruleth well his own house, having his children in subjection with all gravity; [5] (For if a man know not how to rule his own house, how shall he take care of the church of God?) [6] Not a novice, lest being lifted up with pride he fall into the condemnation of the devil. [7] Moreover he must have a good report of them which are without; lest he fall into reproach and the snare of the devil. [8] Likewise *must* the deacons *be* grave, not doubletongued, not given to much wine, not greedy of filthy lucre; [9] Holding the mystery of the faith in a pure conscience. [10] And let these also first be proved; then let them use the office of a deacon, being *found* blameless. [11] Even so *must their* wives *be* grave, not slanderers, sober, faithful in all things. [12] Let the deacons be the husbands of one wife, ruling their children and their own houses well. [13] For they that have used the office of a deacon well purchase to themselves a good degree, and great boldness in the faith which is in Christ Jesus" (I Timothy 3:1-13).

Water baptism connects a believer to the maintenance of the internal purity of his local church by maintaining a formal membership through Congregational Government in accountability of each individual local church member to be involved in aggressive and bold evangelistic outreach. Many local churches are very definitive about what is moral turpitude. However, they become very lax in their faithfulness to the missional purpose of their local church – their own church attendance, their own personal discipleship, and their own efforts in evangelistic outreach.

"[18] And Jesus came and spake unto them, saying, All power is given unto me in heaven and in earth. [19] Go ye therefore, and teach all nations, baptizing them in the name of the Father, and of the Son, and of the Holy Ghost: [20] Teaching them to observe all things whatsoever I have commanded you: and, lo, I am with you alway, *even* unto the end of the world. Amen" (Matthew 28:18-20).

"But ye shall receive power, after that the Holy Ghost is come upon you: and ye shall be witnesses unto me both in Jerusalem, and in the Judea, and in Samaria, and unto the uttermost part of the earth" (Acts 1:8).

"[1] Moreover, brethren, I declare unto you the gospel which I preached unto you, which also ye have received, and wherein ye stand; [2] By which also ye are saved, if ye keep in memory what I preached unto you, unless ye have believed in vain. [3] For I delivered unto {*in the sense of giving something that carries with that giving the responsibility of giving it to others with the same responsibility*} you first of all that which I also received, how that Christ died for our sins according to the scriptures; [4] And that he was buried, and that he rose again the third day according to the scriptures: [5] And that he was seen of Cephas, then of the twelve: [6] After that, he was seen of above five hundred brethren at once; of whom the greater part remain unto this present, but some are fallen asleep. [7] After that, he was seen of James; then of all the apostles. [8] And last of all he was seen of me also, as of one born out of due time. [9] For I am the least of the apostles, that am not meet to be called an apostle, because I persecuted the church of God. [10] But by the grace of God I am what I am: and his grace which *was bestowed* upon me was not in vain; but I laboured more abundantly than they all: yet not I, but the grace of God which was with me. [11] Therefore whether *it were* I or they, so we preach, and so ye believed" (I Corinthians 15:1-11).

Water baptism connects a believer to the maintenance of the internal purity of his local church by maintaining a formal membership through Congregational Government as exemplified in the accountability of each individual local church member in active involvement in the regular assemblies during public times. Unfaithfulness to the assemblies of your local church is unfaithfulness to Christ and manifests disregard for the moral responsibilities testified in a water baptism decision. Congregation Government does not allow mere *lip service* to attendance to the times of assembly.

"Not forsaking the assembling of ourselves together, as the manner of some is; but exhorting one another: and so much the more, as ye see the day approaching" (Hebrews 10:25).

"And upon the first day of the week, when the disciples came together to break bread, Paul preached unto them, ready to depart in the morrow; and continued his speech until midnight" (Acts 20:7).

"Upon the first day of the week let every one of you lay by him in store, as God hath prospered him, that there be no gatherings when I come" (I Corinthians 16:2).

DISCUSSION QUESTIONS

1. Discuss the fact that a local church cannot function the way God intends until they have a proper depth of understanding of the communal decision in water baptism. Also, discuss why it is essential that they have a proper understanding of the *organization* and *organism* of formal membership.

2. Discuss how the seven epistles of Christ to the seven local churches of the book of Revelation define the purpose of biblical separation in maintaining the purity of local churches from false doctrine and worldliness.

3. Discuss Congregational Government's role in maintaining a pure local church, including in your discussion the role water baptism has in this goal.

4. Discuss the view of the Church from Reformed Theology. Discuss why this *Big View* of the Church is contrary and detrimental to maintaining local church purity through separation from false doctrines and worldliness.

5. Read Revelation 22:16 and discuss the significance of the use of word "churches" (plural) rather than the word church (singular).

6. Discuss and explain the difference between the local church during the Church Age and the "general assembly" (Hebrews 12:23) used of the Church in the Kingdom Age.

7. Discuss the six different aspects of the maintenance of the internal purity of a local church to which water baptism connects the believer through Congregational Government and the formal membership of a local church.

BAPTISM
Chapter Thirteen
How Understanding Water Baptism Defines the Personality of a Local Church

It always heart breaking to see children have a difficult beginning in life. Sometimes we might think that certain children would be better off to be born without parents than with the parents that conceived them. These parents have few moral values and little, if any, faith in God. These kinds of parents can barely sustain themselves let alone raise children to believe in God and live for Him. It is tough for children to make it in life when even their parents have no moral compass to guide their decision making.

It has been said that a child learns most of his lifetime values by the time he is five years old. **How you begin is important.** This is also true of a decision to be water baptized. Unless there is a depth of understanding about the way a decision to be water baptized connects to the values of the Christian life, and how that new life is to be lived, that believer will begin his new life with a serious spiritual handicap. Many local churches have such shallow teaching about water baptism, and teaching about the local church, that *newborn* Christians hardly are able to survive when they begin with such shallow roots in their commitments to Christ. Like *foxes in the hen house*, carnality is bound to run rampant in these kinds of local churches.

"[12] For we commend not ourselves again unto you, but give you occasion to glory on our behalf, that ye may have somewhat to *answer* them which glory in appearance, and not in heart. [13] For whether we be beside ourselves, *it is* to God: or whether we be sober, *it is* for your cause. [14] For the love of Christ constraineth us; because we thus judge, that if one died for all, then were all dead: [15] And *that* he died for all, that they which live should not henceforth live unto themselves, but unto him which died for them, and rose again. [16] Wherefore henceforth know we no man after the flesh: yea, though we have known Christ after the flesh, yet now henceforth know we *him* no more. [17] Therefore if any man *be* in Christ, *he is* a new creature: old things are passed away; behold, all things are become new. [18] And all things *are* of

God, who hath reconciled us to himself by Jesus Christ, and hath given to us the ministry of reconciliation; [19] To wit, that God was in Christ, reconciling the world unto himself, not imputing their trespasses unto them; and hath committed unto us the word of reconciliation. [20] Now then we are ambassadors for Christ, as though God did beseech *you* by us: we pray *you* in Christ's stead, be ye reconciled to God. [21] For he hath made him *to be* sin for us, who knew no sin; that we might be made the righteousness of God in him" (II Corinthians 5:12-21).

The truths of II Corinthians 5:14-15 define the intended outcomes of proper teaching regarding water baptism. Teaching a person about the meaning of water baptism is like teaching a child his alphabet. Letters connect to vowels. Vowels connect to word structure. Word structure forms sentences and sentences communicate meaning and ideas. However, without the basics of the alphabet, the latter things are never accomplished. Water baptism is intended to be the transition from a believer's *position* "in Christ" to *practice* of the *Christ-life*. There are three central phrases in II Corinthians 5:14-15 that define the practical lifestyle of a person who genuinely understands his decision in water baptism.

1. "For the love of Christ constraineth us"

"For the love of Christ constraineth us - We have the love of God shed abroad in our hearts, and this causes us to love God intensely, and to love and labor for the salvation of men. And it is the effect produced by this love which συνεχει ημας {*"constraineth us"*}, bears us away with itself, which causes us to love after the similitude of that love by which we are influenced; and as God so loved the world as to give his Son for it, and as Christ so loved the world as to pour out his life for it, so we, influenced by the very same love, desire to spend and be spent for the glory of God, and the salvation of immortal souls. By the fear of God the apostles endeavored to persuade and convince men, and the love of Christ constrained them so to act."[70] Words in { } added.

---

[70] Clarke, Adam. *Adam Clarkes Commentary on the Bible* - II Corinthians 5:14. Grand Rapids: Baker Book House, 1984, SwordSearcher Software 6.1.

2. "[B]ecause we thus judge, that if one died for all, then were all dead"

Undoubtedly, Christ died for all sinners, not merely a select few, as the Calvinists would falsely contend. Therefore, because Christ died for all sinners, all sinners "were dead in trespasses and sins" (Ephesians 2:1). Jesus propitiated God's wrath "for our sins: and not for ours only, but also for *the sins of the whole world*" (I John 2:2). Universal condemnation required the universal propitiation of God's wrath. The idea is that apart from the redemptive work of Jesus Christ and His free offer of salvation, every individual in the world had a sealed destiny of eternal death and separation from God and were without hope in this world (Ephesians 2:12). However, "in Christ" through salvation, every believer is united presently and immediately to the "blessed hope" and the "new creation," opening a door of opportunity to live supernaturally empowered by the indwelling Holy Spirit of God. However, the "born again" believer is not to waste this supernatural potential on selfish pursuits and worldliness.

3. "And *that* he died for all, that they which live should not henceforth live unto themselves, but unto him which died for them, and rose again."

Water baptism is a decision that connects the believer to a radically different way of living. The self-sacrifice of the incarnate Son of God in paying the price of our redemption demands the highest form of self-sacrifice from the believer in living the gift of his new life "in Christ." The intent of this verse is not that we simply give the Lord Jesus our *spare time*. The intent of this verse is not that we add Jesus to our own plans for our life. The intent of this verse is that we abandon our own personal ambitions and plans for our life and add the totality of our existence and potential to the plan of God. That is the decision to which water baptism connects the believer. Anything less is a life of selfish ignorance of both from what you were saved and to what you are saved. If we understand II Corinthians 5:15 correctly, then this takes the believer beyond the failure of mere ignorance to outright rebellion against the Lordship of Jesus Christ. Complete surrender to Jesus is what defines walking "in newness of life" (Romans 6:4).

"[1] Behold, what manner of love the Father hath bestowed upon us, that we should be called the sons of God: therefore the world knoweth us not, because it knew him not. [2] Beloved, now are we the sons of God, and it doth not yet appear what we shall be: but we know that, when he shall appear, we shall be like him; for we shall see him as he is. [3] And every man that hath this hope in him purifieth {*present active indicative*} himself, even as he is pure. [4] Whosoever {*present active participle=habitually*} committeth sin {*habitually*} transgresseth also the law: for sin is the transgression of the law. [5] And ye know that he was manifested to take away our sins; and in him is no sin. [6] Whosoever abideth in him {*habitually*} sinneth {*linear present active indicative*} not: whosoever {*habitually*} sinneth {*linear present active articular participle*} hath not seen him, neither known him. [7] Little children, let no man {*habitually*} deceive {*present active imperative*} you: he that {*habitually*} doeth {*present active participle*} righteousness is righteous, even as he is righteous. [8] He that {*habitually*} committeth sin is of the devil; for the devil sinneth {*linear progressive present active indicative, "the devil has been sinning from the beginning"*} from the beginning. For this purpose the Son of God was manifested, that he might destroy the works of the devil. [9] Whosoever is born of God doth not {*habitually*} commit sin; for his seed remaineth in him: and he cannot sin {*present active infinitive –"he cannot keep on sinning"*}, because he is born of God. [10] In this the children of God are manifest, and the children of the devil: whosoever {*habitually*} doeth {*linear present participle*} not righteousness is not of God, neither he that {*habitually*} loveth {*present active participle*} not his brother" (I John 3:1-10).

There are a number of spiritual factors accomplished in the death, burial, and resurrection of Christ that every believer must understand in order to be saved "by grace through faith." These spiritual factors of the finished, redemptive work of Jesus Christ are what define the Gospel of Jesus Christ. Can someone believe something that he does not understand? If they have no understanding of the basic aspects of Christ's basis of their redemption, have they then believed what they do not understand?   If a person cannot articulate an elementary understanding of redemption, how then can he look backward in testimony through water baptism to something that he does not understand and something he probably does not have – SALVATION? Herein is the ultimate shallowness of a dumbed-down Christianity that fills our local churches with unregenerate people. Is there then any wonder why this kind of *Christianity* is fruitless? We have created hundreds of local churches filled with water baptized *one-two-three, say it after me* people with professions of faith that are lacking in any real understanding of the Gospel.   Then, we ask them to evangelize using the same methodology that brought them to their own false profession of salvation. Show me a professing *Christian* who cannot explain his own salvation and I will show you a lost man. We find this reality in Christ's explanation of His parable regarding the *sower*, the *seed*, and the *soils*. Notice in this text how critical it is to genuine salvation to *understand* the doctrine of salvation. Notice also that there needs to be an understanding of a genuine biblical response to the Gospel - **repentance** of sin and "dead works," **belief** in the Gospel, **confess** Jesus to be God, **call** on the name of Jesus to be saved, and **receive** the indwelling of Jesus in the Person of the Holy Spirit.   It is in a careful examination of the salvation decision where a biblical examination begins to insure a biblical decision in water baptism.

"[19] When any one heareth the word of the kingdom, and underdeth *it* not, then cometh the wicked *one*, and catcheth away that which was sown in his heart. This is he which received seed by the way side. [20] But he that received the seed into stony places, the same is he that heareth the word, and anon with joy receiveth it; [21] Yet hath he not root in himself {*no depth of understanding*}, but dureth for a while: for when tribulation or persecution ariseth because of the word, by and by he is offended. [22] He also that received seed among the thorns is he that heareth the word; and the care of this world, and the deceitfulness of riches, choke the word, {*no genuine repentance and therefore no disconnect from worldliness due to misunderstanding*} and he becometh unfruitful. [23] But he that received seed into the good ground is he that heareth the word, and understandeth *it*; which also beareth fruit, and bringeth forth, some an hundredfold, some sixty, some thirty" (Matthew 13:19-23).

Our beliefs and practices are the determining factors in defining our individual personalities. When we join ourselves individually to another person or group of people, we begin to formulate a *corporate personality*. This is true of a husband and wife relationship, an immediate family relationship, an extended family relationship, and even a local church relationship. A corrupted *corporate personality* of a local church is certainly generated by the shallow presentation of the Gospel, a shallow and insufficient understanding of the Gospel, and a shallow understanding of the commitment to Christ testified to through water baptism.

The *corporate personality* is shaped through something called the *corporate ethic*. A *corporate ethic* is the influence of the beliefs and practices of every individual within the group upon all other individuals within the group. There are those within any group that extend higher levels of influence than do other individuals. These individuals are the leaders in formulating the *corporate personality* of the group. These individuals do not need to be officially recognized by the group as the group's leaders. They simply take these leadership roles based upon the dominance of their own personalities in their influence upon the group. This is why a local church must officially choose its spiritual leaders according to biblical criteria and officially put those leaders at the forefront of their *corporate ethic*. This is an extended aspect of Congregational Government in maintaining its *corporate ethic* in order to affect its *corporate personality*.

What defines the *testimony* of your local church? A testimony is your *reputation*. We might say it like this, if someone were to describe you, your family, or your local church in one sentence, what would that sentence be? We must be careful in answering this question not to answer it according to what we *want* that sentence to say. We must be real and honest about what that sentence is in reality. That *testimony* **is** the *corporate personality* of your local church.

This one sentence description of the testimony of any local church is also an established reality to how others in a community view the reality of what it really means to be a "born again," water baptized, discipled of Jesus Christ. In most cases, a bad testimony can be traced back to a false decision and a broken vow to God involving that person's misunderstanding of water baptism.

The best way to discover the answer to this *question* is to ask the question to others outside of the local church. When we ask this *question*, we must take into account any limited exposure to individuals within the *corporate entity* of the person answering. If the individual's exposure to the *corporate entity* is limited to a good or bad testimony of one individual, his answer will be affected accordingly. If the individual's exposure to the *corporate entity* is limited to a good or bad testimony of one point in exposure to the group, his answer will be affected accordingly. If the individual answering the questions has a bias towards any individual within the group or a doctrinal bias towards the group, his answer will be affected accordingly. Perhaps there is no better text in Scripture that defines God's *intended* testimony of every local church than that of Acts 2:42-47. In these few verses of Scripture, we find *the way it ought to be.*

"[42] And they continued stedfastly in the apostles' doctrine and fellowship, and in breaking of bread, and in prayers. [43] And fear came upon every soul: and many wonders and signs were done by the apostles. [44] And all that believed were together, and had all things common; [45] And sold their possessions and goods, and parted them to all *men*, as every man had need. [46] And they, continuing daily with one accord in the temple, and breaking bread from house to house, did eat their meat with gladness and singleness of heart, [47] Praising God, and having favour with all the people. And the Lord added to the church daily such as should be saved" (Acts 2:42-47).

The word "favour" in Acts 2:47 is from the Greek word *charis* (khar'-ece). This Greek word is usually translated *grace* in our KJV Bibles. The basic definition of the word *charis* is "the divine influence upon the heart, and its reflection in the life."[71]   Therefore, the word cannot be disconnected from the supernatural workings of God through the lives of His "born again" children. **A good testimony does not come *by accident.* A good testimony happens *by purpose.*** A decision to be water baptized is God's intended connecting link to this ongoing supernatural dynamic of spiritual empowerment through habitually dying to the "old man" and habitual, total, absolute yielding to the indwelling Christ. A good testimony will happen *by purpose* only by this truly biblical way. The *purposing of this outcome* is the ultimate decision in water baptism.

"[1] Brethren, if a man be overtaken in a fault {*a side-slip, fall, or failure in judgment*}, ye which are spiritual {*living in the supernatural enabling of the indwelling Spirit of God through His filling*}, restore such an one in the spirit of meekness; considering thyself, lest thou also be tempted. [2] Bear ye one another's burdens {*sharing in the weights and trials of life*}, and so fulfil the law of Christ. [3] For if a man think himself to be something, when he is nothing, he deceiveth himself. [4] But let every man prove his own work, and then shall he have rejoicing in himself alone, and not in another. [5] For every man shall bear his own burden. [6] Let him that is taught in the word communicate {*provide sustaining material support*} unto him that teacheth in all good things. [7] Be not deceived; God is not mocked: for whatsoever a man soweth, that shall he also reap. [8] For he that soweth to his flesh shall of the flesh reap corruption; but he that soweth to the Spirit shall of the Spirit reap life everlasting. [9] And let us not be weary in well doing: for in due season we shall reap, if we faint not. [10] As we have therefore opportunity, let us do good unto all *men*, especially unto them who are of the household of faith" (Galatians 6:1-10).

Every local church is like an individual family in the whole congregation of Israel. The fact that every local church is comprised of "born again" believers who are all priests before God is unique to the New Covenant under the High Priesthood of Jesus Christ. Every individual within a local church family is also united by water baptism in a covenant agreement to live for Jesus as His disciple. This unity in our New Covenant agreement

---

[71] Strong, Augustus. *Strong's Greek Dictionary.* SwordSearcher Software 6.1.

through water baptism is very specific in both its degree and in its responsibilities. Water baptism is the *entrance level* decision in becoming a disciple of Jesus Christ. Salvation is not the entrance level decision to discipleship. If we confuse these two decisions, salvation is *top loaded* with hundreds of "works" expectations. This would completely contradict salvation by grace alone through faith alone. Christ gives numerous expectations of those who decide to become His disciples. These disciple expectations are not part of salvation, but should follow genuine salvation.

"[25] And there went great multitudes with him: and he turned, and said unto them, [26] If any *man* come to me, and hate not his father, and mother, and wife, and children, and brethren, and sisters, yea, and his own life also, he cannot be my disciple. [27] And whosoever doth not bear his cross, and come after me, cannot be my disciple. [28] For which of you, intending to build a tower, sitteth not down first, and counteth the cost, whether he have *sufficient* to finish *it*? [29] Lest haply, after he hath laid the foundation, and is not able to finish *it*, all that behold *it* begin to mock him, [30] Saying, This man began to build, and was not able to finish. [31] Or what king, going to make war against another king, sitteth not down first, and consulteth whether he be able with ten thousand to meet him that cometh against him with twenty thousand? [32] Or else, while the other is yet a great way off, he sendeth an ambassage, and desireth conditions of peace. [33] So likewise, whosoever he be of you that forsaketh not all that he hath, he cannot be my disciple. [34] Salt *is* good: but if the salt have lost his savour, wherewith shall it be seasoned? [35] It is neither fit for the land, nor yet for the dunghill; *but* men cast it out. He that hath ears to hear, let him hear" (Luke 14:25-35).

Therefore, the *corporate personality* of any local church is not merely defined by a regenerate membership all individually baptized by immersion. The *corporate personality* of a local church is defined by a regenerate membership all individually baptized by immersion, **which covenantally connects them to the mutual responsibilities of being disciples of Jesus Christ as defined in Luke 14:25-35**. Like salt that has lost "his savour," apart from this mutual level of commitment to Jesus Christ, any local church "is neither fit for the land, nor yet for the dunghill," but rather to be "cast . . . out" as worthless for the purpose for which she is intended. If these responsibilities of a local church member are not detailed at the time of his instruction about the purpose of water baptism, it is little wonder that many local churches have degenerated into nothing more than *Country Clubs for the Saints*. The reason for this corruption is the failure to define the expectations of being a disciple of Jesus Christ to which all believers are connected when they decide to be water baptized.

Water baptism is an important step towards spiritual maturity. There is no magical conference of grace through the ritual. However, someone must communicate the level of commitment expected of the baptismal candidate preceding the ritual of water baptism. The fact that many people do not realize the expectations of Jesus regarding their decisions to become disciples is an age-old problem. We need only read John chapter twenty-one to see that this problem of misunderstanding responsibilities included seven of Christ's chosen twelve. Judas Iscariot had already betrayed Christ, leaving eleven of the original twelve. Seven of the remaining eleven Apostles returned to being fishermen and began to abandon what Jesus had trained them to do. In John 21:2-4 we read, "[2] There were together Simon Peter, and Thomas called Didymus, and Nathanael of Cana in Galilee, and the *sons* of Zebedee {*James and John*}, and two other of his disciples {*possibly Andrew, Peter's brother who was also a fisherman, and perhaps Philip*}. [3] Simon Peter saith unto them, I go a fishing. [4] They say unto him, We also go with thee." The problem that we find in John chapter twenty-one is not unique to these seven disciples of Jesus Christ. The problem is common to all disciples of Jesus Christ just as is the common solution to this common problem given in John 21:15-19. This text is not just about Peter. This text is about every believer that has made a decision to be a disciple of Jesus Christ.

"[15] So when they had dined, Jesus saith to Simon Peter, Simon, *son* of Jonas, lovest thou me more than these? He saith unto him, Yea, Lord; thou knowest that I love thee. He saith unto him, Feed my lambs. [16] He saith to him again the second time, Simon, *son* of Jonas, lovest thou me? He saith unto him, Yea, Lord; thou knowest that I love thee. He saith unto him, Feed my sheep. [17] He saith unto him the third time, Simon, *son* of Jonas, lovest thou me? Peter was grieved because he said unto him the third time, Lovest thou me? And he said unto him, Lord, thou knowest all things; thou knowest that I love thee. Jesus saith unto him, Feed my sheep. [18] Verily, verily, I say unto thee, When thou wast young, thou girdedst thyself, and walkedst whither thou wouldest: but when thou shalt be old, thou shalt stretch forth thy hands, and another shall gird thee, and carry *thee* whither thou wouldest not. [19] This spake he, signifying by what death he should glorify God. And when he had spoken this, he saith unto him, Follow me" (John 21:15-19).

Although Peter is the primary character in the scene before us, he is just one of many with the same problem. We could spend a great deal of time explaining the details of this portion of Scripture. However, the point is simple – a baptismal decision to become a disciple is not the same as actually doing what you have committed to do. Each of us has been like Peter at some point in our lives and we will probably be there again one day. However, we do not need to let past failures defeat us today. We can ALWAYS begin again! I John 1:9 tells us God is the God of *new beginnings* and a *new beginning* is always available to us.

DISCUSSION QUESTIONS

1. Discuss the importance of properly understanding the depth of commitment intended in water baptism to the beginning of a new life "in Christ."

2. Read II Corinthians 5:12-21. Discuss the intended outcomes of a proper understanding of water baptism that are defined by these few verses of Scripture, especially the three phrases discussed in this chapter.

3. Read I John 3:1-10 and explain the importance of understanding the verb tenses in these verses of Scripture as well as the outcomes of a proper understanding of the application of these verb tenses to the life of a professing believer.

4. List and describe the actions of the five verbs from Scripture that describe a biblical response of faith that are necessary to be "born again."

5. Read Matthew 13:19-23 and discuss the importance of the word "understandeth" that is used a number of times in this text.

6. Discuss the difference between individual personality and corporate personality. Discuss how understanding these terms affects your understanding of the ongoing development of a local church as it grows and adds individuals to its formal membership.

7. Read Galatians 6:1-10 and discuss the ongoing, continuous *spiritual dynamic* within the formal membership of a local church that develops and cultivates the testimony of the *corporate ethic* of that local church.

Bibliography

Alford, Henry. *Alford's Greek Testament*, Volume I – IV. Grand Rapids: Baker Book House, 1980

Armitage, Thomas. *The History of the Baptists, Volumes I & II 1886.* Watertown: Maranatha Press, 1980.

Beasley-Murray, G.R. *Baptism In The New Testament.* Grand Rapids: William B. Eerdmans Publishing Company, 1976.

Bush, L. Russ and Nettles, Tom J. *Baptists and the Bible.* Chicago: Moody Press, 1980.

Clarke, Adam. *Adam Clarke's Commentary on the Bible.* Abridged by Ralph Earle, 1966. Kansas City: Beacon Hill Press, 1984.

Christian, John T. *A History of the Baptists Volumes I & II.* Texarkana: Bogard Press, 1922.

Dowling, Tim, Organizing Ed., Briggs, John H.Y., Wright, David F., and Linder, Robert D., Consulting Ed. *Eerdmans' Handbook to the History of Christianity.* Grand Rapids: Wm. B. Eerdmans Publishing Co., 1987.

Eusebius (translated by G.A. Williamson). *The History of the Church from Christ to Constantine.* New York: Dorset Press, 1984.

Hislop, Alexander. *The Two Babylons or The Papal Worship.* Neptune: Loizeaux Brother Bible Truth Depot, 1858.

Jackson, Jeremy C. *No Other Foundation: The Church Through Twenty Centuries.* Westchester: Cornerstone Books, 1980.

Jordan, Anne Devereaux and J.M. Stifle. *The Baptists.* New York: Hippocrene Books, 1980.

Kent, Homer A. Jr. *The Pastoral Epistles Revised Edition.* Winona Lake: BMH Books, 1986.

Ketchum, Lance T. *Studies In the Book of the Revelation of Jesus Christ.* Doctoral Dissertation to Louisiana Baptist University, 2011.

Kuen, Alfred F. *I Will Build My Church.* Translated by Ruby Lindblabd. Chicago: Moody Press, 1971.

Maring, Norman H. and Winthrop, S. Hudson. *A Baptist Manual of Polity and Practice*. Valley Forge: Judson Press, 1991.

Oesterley, W.E. *The Expositor's Greek Testament* edited by Rev. W. Roberson Nicoll, Five Volumes. Grand Rapids: Wm. B. Eerdmans Publishing Co., 1980.

Orchard, G.H. *A Concise History of Baptists from the Time of Christ Their Founder to the 18th Century.* Texarkana: Bogard Press, 1996.

Newell, William R. *Romans Verse By Verse*. Chicago: Moody Press, 1978.

Newell, William R. *Hebrews Verse By Verse.* Chicago: Moody Press, 1978.

Newell, William R. *The Book of the Revelation.* Chicago: Moody Press, 1978.

Perry, Lloyd M. and Gilbert A. Peterson. *Churches In Crisis.* Chicago: Moody Press, 1981.

Pickering, Ernest. *Biblical Separation.* Schaumburg, IL: Regular Baptist Press, 1979.

Pickering, Ernest. *The Tragedy of Compromise: The Origin and Impact of New Evangelicalism.* Greenville: Bob Jones University Press, 1994.

Robertson, Archibald Thomas. *Word Pictures in the New Testament*, Volume I – VI. Grand Rapids: Baker Book House, 1930.

Thompson, E. Wayne and David L. Cummins. *This Day in Baptist History.* Greenville: Bob Jones University Press, 1993.

Wood, Leon. *A Survey of Israel's History.* Grand Rapids, MI: Zondervon Publishing House, 1978.

Lexicons and Dictionaries

Theological Dictionary of the New Testament, Ten Volumes
Edited by Gerhard Kittel and Gerhard Friedrich. Translated and edited by Geoffrey W. Bromiley.
Wm. B. Eerdmans Publishing Co.,reprinted September 1983

Richards, Lawrence O.
Expository Dictionary of Bible Words
Regency Reference Library
Zondervan Publishing House, 1985

Thayer, Joseph H.
Thayer's Greek English Lexicon of the New Testament
Baker Book House, Fifth Printing March 1980

Unger, Merrill F.
The New Unger's Bible Dictionary
Edited by R.K. Harrison, Howard F. Vos and Cyril J. Barber contributing editors.
Moody Press, Revised and updated 1988

Vine, W. E.
An Expository Dictionary of New Testament Words
Fleming H. Revell Company , Seventeenth impression, 1966

The Zondervan Pictoral Encyclopedia of the Bible, Five Volumes
General Editor: Merrill C. Tenney
Associate Editor: Steven Barabas
Zondervan Publishing House; Fifth Printing 1982

www.ingramcontent.com/pod-product-compliance
Lightning Source LLC
Chambersburg PA
CBHW051834090426
42736CB00011B/1799